Cambridge Elements ☰

Elements in the Philosophy of Science
edited by
Jacob Stegenga
University of Cambridge

T0286907

SCIENCE AND THE PUBLIC

Angela Potochnik
University of Cincinnati

CAMBRIDGE
UNIVERSITY PRESS

Shaftesbury Road, Cambridge CB2 8EA, United Kingdom

One Liberty Plaza, 20th Floor, New York, NY 10006, USA

477 Williamstown Road, Port Melbourne, VIC 3207, Australia

314–321, 3rd Floor, Plot 3, Splendor Forum, Jasola District Centre,
New Delhi – 110025, India

103 Penang Road, #05–06/07, Visioncrest Commercial, Singapore 238467

Cambridge University Press is part of Cambridge University Press & Assessment,
a department of the University of Cambridge.

We share the University's mission to contribute to society through the pursuit of
education, learning and research at the highest international levels of excellence.

www.cambridge.org
Information on this title: www.cambridge.org/9781009475822

DOI: 10.1017/9781009049474

First published 2024

A catalogue record for this publication is available from the British Library.

ISBN 978-1-009-47582-2 Hardback
ISBN 978-1-009-04882-8 Paperback
ISSN 2517-7273 (online)
ISSN 2517-7265 (print)

Cambridge University Press & Assessment has no responsibility for the persistence
or accuracy of URLs for external or third-party internet websites referred to in this
publication and does not guarantee that any content on such websites is, or will
remain, accurate or appropriate.

Science and the Public

Elements in the Philosophy of Science

DOI: 10.1017/9781009049474
First published online: February 2024

Angela Potochnik
University of Cincinnati

Author for correspondence: Angela Potochnik, angela.potochnik@uc.edu

Abstract: Science is a product of society: in its funding, its participation, and its application. This Element explores the relationship between science and the public with resources from philosophy of science. Section 1 defines the questions about science's relationship with the public and outlines science's obligation to the public. Section 2 considers the Vienna Circle as a case study in how science, philosophy, and the public can relate very differently than they do at present. Section 3 examines how public understanding of science can have a variety of different goals and introduces philosophical discussions of scientific understanding as a resource. Section 4 addresses public trust in science, including responding to science denial. Section 5 turns to expanded participation in science and considers how this can contribute to public trust in science. Finally, Section 6 draws on earlier sections to cast light on how science might discharge its obligations to the public.

Keywords: public understanding of science, trust in science, public engagement with science, science and society, participatory research, citizen science, diversity in science

ISBNs: 9781009475822 (HB), 9781009048828 (PB), 9781009049474 (OC)
ISSNs: 2517-7273 (online), 2517-7265 (print)

Contents

1 Introduction

The campus of the US National Institutes of Health (NIH), located in Bethesda, MD, is over 300 acres with more than 75 buildings. But this expansive campus is, of course, not even close to being the entirety of the NIH. More than 80 percent of NIH-supported research is conducted by researchers employed by other institutions, spread around the United States and the globe. The NIH's 2023 budget totaled just under 50 billion USD. The US's National Science Foundation had a 2023 budget of nearly 10 billion USD. National and international research councils such as these exist around the world and constitute a primary approach to public investment in scientific and technological research.

At this stage in history, public investment in science is enormous. Beyond monetary investment in scientific research, there is also tremendous social investment in STEM (science, technology, engineering, and mathematics) education and workforce development. In the United States and many other countries, much attention is focused on K-12 science standards, which are reassessed regularly and drive curricular choices and the development of educational resources. Science education is widely viewed as valuable for all students regardless of whether they pursue a STEM career (Feinstein, 2011). According to the PEW Research Center, the number of STEM bachelor's degrees awarded by US institutions grew by 62 percent between 2010 and 2018. The motivation for this public investment, as stated in the 2021 Progress Report for the Federal STEM Education Strategic Plan issued by the US Federal Government (Office of Science and Technology Policy, (2021, 1), is that: "A well-prepared and diverse STEM workforce is essential to maintaining global leadership as it galvanizes the ingenuity of Americans to accelerate tomorrow's breakthroughs and strengthens our economic and national security."

A recent illustration of this commitment is that the CHIPS and Science Act, signed into US law in 2022 and focused primarily on supporting the US semiconductor industry, also authorizes 13 billion USD over five years for STEM education.

This public investment in scientific research, education, and workforce reflects the central societal role science is broadly taken to have. The conduct of scientific research – basic and applied, natural, social, medical, technological, and engineering – is seen to be of crucial importance for public health, economic growth, and societal development.

And yet, as science has become ever-more embedded in the fabric of contemporary human life over the past centuries, it has also become less accessible to human intellects. This applies to members of the public who are not specialists in science and to members of the scientific establishment alike. In the nineteenth century, as the number of people participating in science increased dramatically, scientific research became more specialized and divided into discipline-based academic societies and specialist journals (Fyfe, 2017). Ever since, amassing scientific knowledge has resulted in the increasing importance of specialization and the narrowing of specialties, so that scientific findings are interpretable by an increasingly narrow slice of the population. Even as human health, technology, and daily life are ever-more supported by scientific research, that research is conducted out of view of more and more human minds.

The combination of science's prominent societal position, its recognized value to society, and its inaccessibility has generated broad, continuing interest in the relationship between science and the public. Academic and popular discussions target the role of science in contemporary society, science's role in public policy, public understanding of and trust in science, the effectiveness of science education, the development of the next generation of scientists, and more. Often, these discussions do not simply aim to describe the situation but to raise the alarm: Is science, and the right kinds of science, receiving enough support? Is public policy sufficiently grounded in scientific knowledge? Does the public understand science well enough; is there eroding trust in science? Will the next generation know enough and care enough to become scientists?

The academic discipline of philosophy of science is also increasingly engaged with these and related questions. Over the past several decades, feminist work in philosophy of science has investigated how science is shaped by social values, or what a community takes to be desirable or worthy of pursuit, which often involves moral judgments. This has led to much broader consideration of how values do, and should, influence scientific research. Largely stemming from this focus on the role of values in science (see *Values in Science* in this Element series: Elliott, 2022), philosophers have also begun to investigate how science relates to societal needs, the nature of public distrust in science and why science deserves public trust, public participation in science, and more. In this Element, I explore these and other topics regarding the relationship science bears to the public, primarily from a philosophical perspective and with reference to research in philosophy of science. Along the way, I attend to the role philosophy of science plays – or might play – in theorizing the relationship between science and the public and in discharging science's obligations to the public (see Fehr and Plaisance, 2010; Cartieri and Potochnik, 2013).

I begin, in this introductory section, by clarifying the contours of the project of theorizing the relationship between science and the public (Section 1.1), outlining what I take to be a collective obligation the scientific establishment bears to public institutions and communities (Section 1.2), and introducing the idea of public engagement with science (Section 1.3).

1.1 How to Ask about Science's Relationship to the Public

The first March for Science was held on Earth Day – April 22, 2017 – in Washington, DC and more than 600 other cities around the world. Global attendance was estimated to exceed one million people. The march was intended to reflect popular interest in science and science-based public policy, especially in reaction to the early months of Donald Trump's presidency of the United States. March for Science has since become a nonprofit organization and social media presence with over one million followers.

This suggests a widely shared sense that science is important to public life and public policy – and also a widely shared sense that that importance is in question or under threat. The precise nature of the relationship between science and public life and policy – or, really, of the various relationships science bears to the public – is the broad focus of this Element.

We have already touched on some of the relationships between science and the public; let us articulate that variety in a bit more detail. First, every member of contemporary society engages with products developed on the basis of scientific research, from things as basic as food supplies and medical care to technological innovations and energy supplies. Second, less tangibly but just as significantly, people are subject to laws, policy, and a broad range of other social norms that are based at least in part on scientific findings, from legislation enacting climate mitigation measures to stock market trading, banking regulations, and driving speed limits. Third, most people also have – to some extent – access to and understanding of knowledge gained through science. This access and understanding is mainly via formal education in science, since science is broadly taken to be an educational priority; but scientific knowledge is also accessed via informal educational opportunities, such as in institutions like museums, zoos, and observatories. Fourth, at least some members of the public can access pathways into participation in science. Creating pathways into scientific careers is a main priority of formal K-12 education in science. Note that scientific careers are much broader than university scientists: these also include roles such as lab techs and a wide range of careers in medicine, engineering, technology, agriculture, and more. If one includes the full variety of occupations requiring STEM knowledge and expertise, 23 percent of the total US workforce in 2019 was in STEM careers (Okrent and Burke, 2021).[1]

---

[1] A note on terminology: I employ an expansive rather than a limited conception of science in this Element. The acronym "STEM" has become a common signifier of speaking broadly about science. I use this acronym when addressing topics where this phrasing is common – for example, STEM careers – but I intend a broad conception of science throughout.

To summarize, everyone participating in contemporary society uses products and is subject to laws and norms based in part on scientific research; most have some exposure to scientific knowledge and many have access to professional pathways into STEM careers. These four types of relationship between science and the public are depicted in Figure 1. Each of these relationships, and probably others as well, can be investigated under the heading of science and the public. Indeed, all of these are subject to investigation. Science policy investigates and advocates the use of science in policymaking (e.g. Gaiek et al., 2020). I have already discussed the significant societal attention placed on broad-based science education and pathways into STEM careers. There is also a significant amount of work addressing inequities in access to STEM careers. And, perhaps more than any of these other targets, there is attention to how scientific findings can lead to commercialization opportunities, medical advances, and other practical effects for human lives – and to how those effects can be improved and made more equitable.

It is worth noting also that targets for investigations about science and the public include both descriptions of science's actual relevance for and relationship to the public, as well as normative claims about what these should be. Descriptive investigations about science and the public aim to accurately characterize how science and the public in fact relate to or influence one another. Normative investigations about science and the public aim instead to characterize how science and the public *should* relate to or influence one another. Thus one might investigate, for example, whether a proposed policy is in fact backed by the latest relevant scientific research (descriptive investigation) or how scientific research might more effectively shape policy (normative investigation). Or one might investigate

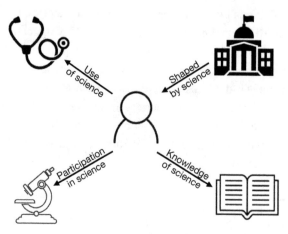

Figure 1 Four types of relationship between science and the public.

public understanding of science and how it changes over time (descriptive investigation) or the proper goals and methods of science education (normative investigation). These different projects, require different areas of expertise and methods, including different forms of empirical research and theory development.

Another variation in targets for investigations about science and the public is *who* is taken to be the relevant public. One question is regarding the scale of investigation: one might focus on (one variety or another of) scientific relationship for whole societies, specific institutions or communities, or individual people – individuals in general or with specified features. With these delineations, I don't mean to indicate the number of individuals targeted but rather the scale of the social group or institution targeted for descriptive or normative investigation to provide understanding or support intervention. For example, the focus might be science curricula across nations (societal); access to health information in US Latino communities (community); or depth of scientific understanding for the average US resident (individual people). Another question about the targeted public is in regard to its demographic features. Features like nationality, age, race, education level, religious affiliation, citizenship status, and linguistic background can be highly relevant to relationships between the public and science. Sometimes such demographic features are focal to an investigation; in other instances they are neglected entirely, resulting in an implicit focus on some limited segment of the public.

1.2 What Science Owes

Recall the description at the start of this section of the tremendous public investment in science worldwide via national and international research councils and the pride of place afforded STEM education and workforce development. Both reflect science's privileged societal position, or societal investment (where "investment" is broader than just monetary support).

This societal investment relates in part to science's social value: the practical and epistemic value science has for society. Science has developed methods and institutions that provide the best systematic approaches yet invented to generating epistemic goods. What I call "epistemic goods" include knowledge of our world and its behaviors, predictions of what to expect in novel situations, practical abilities of intervention and invention, and understanding of a virtually limitless range of phenomena.

Yet, alongside societal investment and its social value, science has also contributed to social problems. Throughout its history and up to the present, science has not only reflected but also contributed to social inequality along the dimensions of race, gender, nationality, and more. These contributions take many forms, including who participates in the institution of science and the focus of research agendas. The historic development of the institutions of science is inextricably intertwined with colonialism, and professional participation in science remains disproportionately European and North American, affluent, white, and male. Meanwhile, scientific research agendas often reflect the values and concerns of their dominant practitioners. Beyond this, scientific research has too often contributed to social inequality through how research is conducted, exploiting or even abusing underserved communities in the process, or through what the research aims to accomplish, such as widespread research, extending into the present, exploring whether there are race, class, or gender differences in cognitive ability. Science has also arguably contributed to other social problems, perhaps in its application in war technologies or other problematic research-based innovations.

These three aspects of science's relationship to society – its societal investment, its societal value, and its contributions to social problems – are the kinds of properties often considered to generate obligations. Science's societal investment is a benefit it has received from society. Science's practical and epistemic value is a capacity it possesses to contribute to society. And science's contributions to social problems are debts it owes to society. In virtue of what it has received, what it can contribute, and the wrongs in which it has participated, the institution of science has special obligations to society. I define this obligation as follows:

Science's Obligation to the Public: Science, as an institution, has an obligation to engineer its relationship to public institutions and communities in virtue of its societal investment, its societal value, and its contributions to social problems.

A consideration of each part of this claim can yield insight into the nature of the obligation. First, what science owes to the public can be clarified by considering the sources I have posited for this obligation: *science's societal investment, societal value, and contributions to social problems*. In virtue of what science has received from society, its societal investment, science owes to society the outcomes those investments are intended to produce. I've mentioned two forms of societal investment: monetary investment in scientific research and educational investment. The former seems intended to produce advances of worth to society, while the latter seems intended to produce broad access to career pathways in science (whether or not such pathways are pursued) and to what is epistemically and practically valuable about science (such as knowledge of important findings and skills from science that are widely applicable). In virtue of what science is best positioned to contribute to society, its societal value, it owes those contributions – be they knowledge or products – that advance society's best interests. Notice that, on the view I am sketching, science's societal value is a source of obligation as well as something that is owed, insofar as science is obligated to develop knowledge and products that advance society's best interests. Finally, in virtue of science's contributions to social problems, it owes its involvement in ameliorating those problems. So, for its contributions to social inequality of various forms, the institution of science should participate in ameliorating relevant social inequalities. And, similarly, science should work to ameliorate any detrimental effects of its innovations. All this is summarized in Table 1.

How these various sources of societal obligation each gives rise to different kinds of societal obligations could be analyzed in much greater depth, but I will add just a bit more nuance to this initial introduction. One important point is that this analysis of how science's societal investment, societal value, and contributions to social problems each generates particular types of obligations suggests that the nature of obligation may vary with the circumstances. Perhaps, for example, greater educational investment gives rise to a greater obligation to generate career pathways and public access to valuable knowledge and skills from science. Science's obligations to society might in turn shape the nature of societal investment.[2] For example, perhaps societal investment should be directed specifically to support public trust in science. It is interesting to note that

Table 1 Relationships among the sources of science's societal obligations, and the nature of those obligations.

Source of obligation	Variety of source	Type of obligation
Societal investment	Monetary investment in research	Advances of societal worth
	Educational investment	Career pathways; public access to science's value, such as knowledge and skills
Societal value	Epistemic value	Knowledge and products that advance society's best interests;
	Practical value	cultivating trustworthiness
Contributions to social problems	Social inequality	Ameliorating inequalities
	Problematic innovations	Ameliorating detrimental effects

---

[2] Conversation with Eduardo Martinez.

monetary and educational investment in science do at least sometimes align with the related obligations posited here, such as when grants prioritize societal impact and when educational resources are directed at the STEM career pipeline. One also might wonder whether, to the extent that science discharges its obligations to society, it is owed societal investment. I leave open that question here.

Second, I have claimed that science's obligation to the public is an obligation of science, *as an institution*. This can clarify what entities or individuals bear the obligation. Obligations to the public do not stem from science simply as a set of epistemic practices but to the institutions of science as they have developed in their social and cultural contexts. Different institutions and disciplinary fields of science may vary in their obligations depending on, for example, past contributions to social harms or the extent of societal investment. Indeed, science's obligation may obtain to and be best discharged by a range of disciplines, including what we might call science-adjacent fields like philosophy of science. The extent and nature of the obligation depend on a discipline's societal investment, societal value, and contributions to social problems. A discipline's usefulness to discharging science's societal obligations may provide prudential grounds for increasing societal investment, or its share of science's societal investment, so the discipline is better able to assist in discharging science's societal obligations.

Insofar as these obligations apply to the institutions of science, they primarily constitute collective rather than individual obligations (Douglas, 2013). Scientific institutions collectively (and variously) have obligations to society; any obligations of individuals stem from their roles in those institutions. I will not take a position here on whether, to what extent, and in what ways individual scientists and other participants in science's institutions inherit these obligations. If individuals do inherit science's obligation to the public, the nature and extent of obligation surely depends on individuals' roles – for example, a graduate student or an officer of a funding agency; a prominent, well-supported senior scientist in the UK or a scientist struggling to establish themselves in a more challenging institutional or national context. Individual scientists are, of course, bound by norms of research ethics, as are scientific institutions. Science's obligation to the public, as discussed here, may influence research ethics but it goes beyond typical articulations of those norms, the latter of which focus primarily on the treatment of research subjects and, potentially, societal implications of research (Shrader-Frechette, 1994; Douglas, 2009). Douglas (2022) points out that research ethics norms provide baseline obligations that all researchers must adhere to, while societal responsibility is better articulated as goals to aim for.

Third, my generic statement of science's obligation to the public is an obligation *to engineer science's relationship to public institutions and communities.* "Engineering" here is meant to evoke conscious design. Scientific institutions are organized to advance scientific inquiry and shape inquiry according to applicable moral values, and it has been suggested that semiorganized or unorganized groups in science also collectively bear epistemic responsibility (Fleisher and Šešelja, 2023). I suggest that scientific institutions and less formal scientific groups, like disciplinary fields, are also bound by directly public-oriented obligations. Some of these obligations regard epistemic responsibility and the responsible conduct of research, while others related to science education, trustworthiness, and career pathways go beyond research activities. Crucially, fulfilling the obligations arising variously from societal investment, societal value, and contribution to social problems requires knowing what is good for or of value to society; how to support career pathways and trustworthiness; and evaluating social problems and how to address them. Such knowledge requires public input of various kinds, as well as support from other disciplines, such as ethical and political analysis. There is thus a need for the institutions of science to invest effort and research into science's relationship with the public to discern the specific nature of what it owes and to arrange itself to fulfill those obligations.

1.3 Public Engagement with Science

Science's obligation to the public, as developed in the previous section, relates not just to how scientific research is conducted but also to how that research is responsive to public concern and societal needs, as well as to how public institutions and communities relate to scientific research and its products. Discharging this obligation thus must involve more than simply conducting scientific research in the proper way. I want to suggest the phrase *public engagement with science* as a broad, umbrella category for any and all interfaces between science and public institutions and communities. The active and creative management of these interfaces – effective public engagement with science – is an important tool for discharging science's obligation to the public. As I have phrased this obligation, science as an institution is obligated to engineer its relationship to public institutions and communities. The interfaces between science and public institutions and communities, such as science education, scientific research in communities, and science policy, offer key opportunities to engineer science's relationship to the public.

The contours of science's obligation to the public can provide insight into the variety of targeted groups, activities, and goals within the umbrella category of public engagement with science. First, public engagement with science projects may target a range of different segments of the public, including different communities as well as public institutions. Science's obligation to the public does not solely bear on its relationships to other societal institutions but also to a variety of communities. Considering the variety and sources of science's obligation to the public indicated in Section 1.2 and summarized in Table 1, communities of relevance include any communities indirectly investing in science (e.g. through taxes or time), that stand to gain epistemically or practically from science, or that suffer from difficulties to which science has contributed. So, high school students are a relevant community, as are US taxpayers, a community suffering health effects from environmental pollution, members of a minoritized group targeted in past scientific research that is now recognized to be racist, and many more besides.

Second, a wide variety of activities targeting different interfaces between science and the public may productively contribute to public engagement with science. The variety includes public-oriented science communication, formal and informal science education, science policy, public participation in scientific research, and more. As this suggests, I consider engagement with social institutions, as in much science policy work, to constitute public engagement with science as well. Sometimes public engagement is thought to require engagement with the wider public – that is, with individuals without relevant expertise – but I prefer using "public engagement with science" as a broader umbrella term. Similar aims might be served by engagement with social institutions as with community engagement, even if the methods vary. Third, the goals of public engagement with science also vary widely, ranging from increased scientific understanding to improved trust in science or increased basis for trust, cultivating a sense of connection and belonging in science, improved responsiveness of scientific research to a community's concerns, and more.

As briefly indicated, science's obligation to the public is also best discharged by a range of disciplines, including what we might call science-adjacent fields like philosophy of science and fields that may not target science directly but have resources that might be brought to bear. Philosophy of science can help respond to science's obligation to the public in part by theorizing the relationship between science and the public, as in this Element and much research by other authors, a sampling of which is discussed in the pages that follow. But that is not the only valuable contribution from philosophy of science. Philosophers of science also engage – and might engage more fully – by direct involvement in public outreach initiatives and training. Fehr and Plaisance (2010) outline these various forms of public engagement by philosophers, while Conix et al. (2022) summarize their features and report research bearing on the extent to which they are conducted by philosophers.

I conjecture that public engagement with science is most effectively conducted as (1) an interdisciplinary, (2) community-engaged endeavor where (3) the multidirectional forms of influence between science and relevant public institutions and communities are attended to. Skills and bodies of knowledge from a range of disciplines bear on effectively evaluating and responding to science's obligation to the public, and community concerns and values must shape the nature of public engagement of science for it to be effective. Further, as my discussion of science's obligation to the public makes clear, the aims of public engagement with science include not just changes to public institutions or communities, such as greater trust in science, but also changes to the institutions of science, such as greater trustworthiness. (See Potochnik and Jacquart, forthcoming, for a much deeper discussion of these three themes.)

The point about multidirectional influences deserves emphasis. Public engagement with science, as defined here, cannot consist in mere science boosterism. The project is not simply to help audiences outside science better appreciate science's wonders or increase their allegiance to STEM institutions and initiatives. I have introduced public engagement with science as the interfaces between science and public institutions and communities, the active and creative management of which can help discharge science's obligation to the public. The ultimate goal of public engagement with science is not increased support for and acceptance of science, but for the institutions of science to compensate for the significant societal investment they receive, the significant societal goods they can produce, and the injustices and social problems to which they have contributed.

1.4 What's to Come

The focus of this Element is not primarily developing an account of science's obligation to the public or a conception of public engagement with science but rather broadly exploring philosophical work on some of the main interfaces between science and the public. For this reason, the focus will expand in the following several sections. I return to the idea of science's obligation to the public in Section 6.

In Section 2, I discuss the Vienna Circle, an influential philosophical group in the early twentieth century, as a model of how the interrelationships among philosophy of science, the sciences, and the public might differ from their present version. I do not suggest this as a goal state to return to but simply put the model forward to illustrate the potential for radically different interrelationships among academic and public institutions. In Section 3, I engage with the topic of public understanding of science, first by examining what is taken to be

important to and important about understanding science and, then, by considering how philosophical investigations of scientific understanding can inform this
topic. In Section 4, I consider the issue of public trust in science, which is
distinct from public understanding of science and arguably more important.
I begin by surveying accounts of science denial and of science's epistemic
authority – reasons why the public *should* trust science – then move on to the
challenge posed by warranted distrust in science and proposals for how we
might meet that thornier challenge. In Section 5, I address participation in
science: both the diversity of professional STEM practitioners and the inclusion
of nonspecialists in scientific research. I explore how expanding participation in
science may be able to contribute to public trust in science.

Finally, in Section 6, I return to science's obligation to the public, outlined in
this section, to explore how expanded participation in science may offer a route
to a science more responsive to the public that, ultimately, could assist science's
ability to discharge its obligation to the public. Discussions in Sections 2–5
provide resources for the various obligations that, I have suggested, comprise
science's obligation to the public (summarized in Table 1). The investigation in
Section 3 of public understanding of science shows how science education
might be shaped to better address science's obligations to provide public access
to science's value, such as knowledge and skills. The discussion in Section 4 of
public trust in science and warranted distrust of science reveals some contours
of how greater trustworthiness of science might be cultivated. Section 5
explores how expanded participation in science can be recruited to support
many if not all of science's various obligations to the public. These include
science's ability to provide advances of societal worth, such as knowledge and
products that advance society's best interests, ameliorating social inequalities
and social problems, and ultimately increasing science's trustworthiness.
Diversified professional participation in science is also important to equitably
providing career pathways in STEM. Finally, Section 2 suggests ways in which
philosophy of science might relate differently to science, to the public, and to
the relationships thereof, which supports Section 6's concluding consideration
of how philosophers of science are well positioned to contribute to discharging
science's obligation to the public.

Thus, Sections 2–5 provide theoretical resources for the various aspects of
science's obligation to the public. But that is not the only purpose of those
sections. Even if one does not subscribe to this statement of science's obligation
to the public, the interfaces between science and the public explored in this
Element are worthy of study. The broad contours of how philosophy, science,
and the public interrelate; public understanding of science; public trust in
science; and participation in science are topics worthy of investigation and to

which research in philosophy of science can meaningfully contribute. Similarly, the list of obligations summarized in Table 1 are widely held goals, even if they are not always thought to be obligations. Beyond the specific views outlined, this Element aims to help locate science and the public as a distinct topic of philosophical inquiry and to bring philosophical research that bears on this topic more fully into that conversation.

2 The Vienna Circle: A Different Model of Philosophy, Science, and the Public

In the early twentieth century, the Great War – World War I – led to the end of the Ottoman and Austro-Hungarian empires and the founding of several new nation states. Einstein's advances in physics led to a radical revision of our understanding of light, gravity, and the very nature of space and time. And the artistic and cultural movements of modernism rejected traditional forms of art, architecture, music, and social organization to instead explore and experiment with their structure. The city of Vienna directly felt many of these transformations: downgraded from the capital of the sprawling Austro-Hungarian Empire to the overly cosmopolitan capital of the small, newly created nation of Austria; home to mathematicians and psychologists transforming their fields; and undergoing rapid artistic, architectural, and social change.

It was in this context that a circle of academics trained variously in physics, mathematics, philosophy, economics, and sociology began to meet weekly in 1923. Invitations to the meetings were issued by Moritz Schlick, the chair for natural philosophy at the University of Vienna, trained in both physics and philosophy and known for his book, *Space and Time in Contemporary Physics*, which addressed the philosophical implications of Einstein's and Planck's breakthroughs in physics. Active in the group from its beginning were Hans Hahn, a mathematician who had helped bring Schlick to Vienna; Philipp Frank, a physicist; and Otto Neurath, an economist and sociologist active in politics. (These three had also convened regular meetings about science and philosophy in Vienna from 1907 to 1912.) In the decade or so over which regular meetings of the Vienna Circle were held, the Circle had a shifting membership of about ten to eighteen people, with students and intellectuals arriving and departing Vienna, as well as a rotating cast of visitors from abroad (Stadler, 2007). Philosopher Rudolf Carnap began visiting the Circle in 1924 and took up a position in Vienna in 1926. In 1929, about six years after the Circle began, Schlick declined a job offer at another university. In celebration, Neurath, Carnap, Hahn, and others coauthored a piece describing the ambitious, programmatic agenda of the group (Hahn et al., 1929). It was in this piece, which they dubbed their "manifesto," that the group was first named the "Vienna Circle."[3]

Shortly before this, in 1927, a radical socialist organization, the Austrian Freethinkers, formed the Ernst Mach Society. Its namesake, Mach, had been a physicist and philosopher, Schlick's predecessor as the chair of natural philosophy at the University of Vienna; its aim was to provide science education to a broad public audience. When the Society was launched, Schlick was named its president, with Hahn vice president and Neurath and Carnap its secretaries. They regularly organized public talks, with speakers including members of the Vienna Circle, as well as notable figures in Vienna's left political movement. Between the World Wars Vienna was run by a socialist government, the Social Democratic Workers' Party (SDAP), with an ideology known as Austro-Marxism. Neurath was a leader in the ambitious public housing movement at the heart of the SDAP, working with modernist architects Adolf Loos and Josef Frank; the latter was also the brother of Vienna Circle member Philipp Frank. From 1925, Neurath also ran The Museum of Society and Economy, which used pictures to represent important statistics about modern life to the working-class people of Vienna.

Several participants in the Vienna Circle, and the philosophical movement of logical empiricism it promoted, were foundational for today's anglophone philosophy of science. And yet, even in this brief account, several aspects of the relationship the Vienna Circle's philosophy bears to science and to the public stand out as different from today. The Circle was a multidisciplinary group – indeed, a group composed even of multidisciplinary individuals, moving variously among philosophy, mathematics, physics, psychology, economics, and sociology. Several members of the Vienna Circle actively produced public talks and popular writings; indeed, there was less of a distinction between their academic and popular writing than is typical today. Finally, the Vienna Circle was in conversation with other important intellectual and cultural movements afoot, from the Austro-Marxism ideology of the SDAP to Alfred Adler's and Sigmund Freud's theoretical work in psychology and the Bauhaus school of modernist art, design, and architecture. Each of these parties expressed a sense that these movements in philosophy, politics, science, and art were interrelated.

In light of these differences between early twentieth-century Vienna and today, this section explores what we can learn from the Vienna Circle and its cultural context as a model of the relationships among philosophy, science, and the public. I will not draw any direct conclusions from this case study about how science and its philosophy should relate to the public. Rather, I introduce this alternative

---

[3] Much of this summary relies on Edmonds (2020), a very good overview of the history of the Vienna Circle, including its philosophical and social context.

model to inspire more openness to what these relationships might entail. The example of the Vienna Circle demonstrates that our current milieu for thinking about science and the public is not inevitable – and has in fact been different in the past. In Section 2.1, I examine the relationship between philosophy and science in the Vienna Circle. In Section 2.2, I consider the continuity between the philosophical projects of the Vienna Circle – and of the Ernst Mach Society – and their cultural and political projects. Finally, in Section 2.3, I suggest that the Vienna Circle's logical empiricism was ultimately a political stance, and I survey how that changed with the death or emigration of its members in ways that deeply affected its legacy in contemporary anglophone philosophy.

2.1 Philosophy Embedded in Science

In the manifesto published in 1929, the Vienna Circle outlined their broad orientation to philosophy, though there was always a healthy dose of disagreement among the members of the Circle on any given detail. This orientation, and the title of their manifesto, was *wissenschaftliche Weltauffassung*, typically translated as "scientific conception of the world." The manifesto contrasts this orientation with "metaphysical and theologising thought [on the rise] not only in life but also in science" (Hahn et al., 1929, 301). The formation of the Vienna Circle is described as follows:

> Around Schlick, there gathered in the course of time a circle whose members united various endeavours in the direction of a scientific conception of the world. This concentration produced a fruitful mutual inspiration. Not one of the members is a so-called "pure" philosopher; all of them have done work in a special field of science. Moreover they come from different branches of science and originally from different philosophic attitudes. But over the years a growing uniformity appeared; this too was a result of the specifically scientific attitude . . . if there are differences of opinion, it is in the end possible to agree, and therefore agreement is demanded. (Hahn et al., 1929, 304)

The work of the Vienna Circle has become historically important in philosophy, especially in philosophy of science, but they thought of their work as opposed to traditional philosophy, and the thinkers in the Circle were at a remove from the institutional power of philosophy in Vienna. The University of Vienna's philosophy department largely focused on the history of philosophy rather than on science. The professors were conservative, rarely interacting with students. Several members of the Vienna Circle were not salaried faculty but rather *Privatdozent*, who were permitted to teach classes but not paid a salary.[4]

Further, as noted in the passage quoted, the training of many members of the Vienna Circle included more mathematics, physics, and other sciences than it

---

[4] This discussion follows Edmonds (2020) unless otherwise noted.

did philosophy, and their intellectual orbits reflected this as well. The physicist Ernst Mach's positivism was perhaps the greatest influence on the views of the Vienna Circle. Schlick completed a doctorate in physics under physicist Max Planck, and he then authored a book grappling with the philosophical implications of Einstein's breakthroughs in physical theory, which was well received in general and taken up with interest by Einstein. Einstein also followed the work of Philip Frank, and he became close friends with both Schlick and Frank. When Einstein moved on from the German University of Prague, he recommended Frank as his replacement as the chair of theoretical physics.

As this suggests, the work of Schlick, Frank, and other members of the Vienna Circle was valued by physicists of the day for its scientific importance. The new breakthroughs in theoretical physics, both Einstein's relativity and quantum theories, were recognized as deeply philosophical. Einstein's theory of general relativity posited non-Euclidean geometry, in direct violation of the Kantian view that Euclidean geometry is a synthetic a priori truth. As Friedman (2007) discusses, "these problems in the foundations of geometry and physics were intimately intertwined with issues in the philosophy (and psychology) of sense perception and thus with more general issues in the epistemology of empirical knowledge" (92). The Vienna Circle's contributions to theoretical physics and their contributions to these topics in philosophy were thus one and the same.

Beyond physics, several members of the Vienna Circle were also trained in and made contributions to mathematics, economics, and sociology. Some members, most prominently Kurt Gödel, contributed to the foundations of mathematics. Karl Menger worked in mathematics and economics, contributing to the beginnings of rational choice theory; Neurath was an economist and a social scientist; Felix Kaufmann was active in sociology; and Edgard Zilsel worked on the sociology of knowledge, including the sciences (Uebel, 2007; Edmonds, 2020). Some members of the Vienna Circle also engaged seriously with theoretical advances in psychology, including Sigmund Freud's psychoanalysis and Alfred Adler's holistic Gestalt psychology. In biology, Ludwig von Bertalanffy, a founder of systems theory, was a student of Schlick, Carnap, and Neurath, and J. H. Woodger, a prominent British biologist, collaborated with Neurath and Carnap (Hofer, 2002).

At this time, there was thus a great deal of continuity between philosophy and the various sciences. Students were often trained in several disciplines, even in their advanced studies, and scholars moved between science and philosophy with relative ease. Significant research topics were seen as relevant in both science and philosophy of science. A vivid illustration of this continuity is provided by the various conferences the Vienna Circle organized, from the First Conference for the Epistemology of the Exact Sciences in 1929 through the Sixth (and final) International Congress for the Unity of Science held in

1941. These conferences included not just philosophers of science but mathematicians, physicists, and other scientists as well. For instance, at the Second International Congress, Gödel presented his famous incompleteness theorem in logic, while the physicist Niels Bohr presented his views on the complementary perspectives of light as wave and as particle (Werkmeister, 1936).

This continuity between philosophy and the sciences in the Vienna Circle extended also to their pattern of work, which they viewed as cooperative and incremental in opposition to past philosophical system building. The passage quoted from their manifesto (Hahn et al., 1929, 304) emphasizes "growing uniformity" across their views. While the members of the Vienna Circle never agreed on any main points of discussion, they often took pains to emphasize the broad points of agreement among them rather than the aspects of disagreement. In the introduction to the first edition of his book *Der Logische Aufbau der Welt*, Carnap contrasts the "spectacle . . . [of] a multiplicity of incompatible philosophical systems" to a philosophy patterned instead after the sciences:

> If we allot to the individual in philosophical work as in the special sciences only a partial task, then we can look with more confidence into the future: in slow careful construction insight after insight will be won. Each collaborator contributes only what he can endorse and justify before the whole body of his co-workers. Thus stone will be carefully added to stone and a safe building will be erected at which each following generation can continue to work. (Carnap, 1928, xvii)

2.2 Philosophy of the Cultural and Political Moment

The Vienna Circle's manifesto described in the previous section was dedicated to the Ernst Mach Society. Recall that this society aimed to provide science education to a broad audience and its leaders were all members of the Vienna Circle. The society organized public talks, some with members of the Vienna Circle or other prominent scientists as speakers, others featuring important individuals in Austro-Marxism. The manifesto specifies:

> The Vienna Circle believes that in collaborating with the Ernst Mach Society it fulfils a demand of the day: we have to fashion intellectual tools for everyday life, for the daily life of the scholar but also for the daily life of all those who in some way join in working at the conscious re-shaping of life. (Hahn et al., 1929, 305)

So, members of the Vienna Circle not only saw their philosophical work as continuous with the sciences; they also saw it as continuous with contributions to social change. In the Vienna Circle, we see philosophers of science fully participating, as philosophers, in their cultural and political moment. The manifesto says, of the alignment between these projects, that "endeavours toward a new organization of economic and social relations, toward the unification of mankind, toward a reform of school and education, all show an inner link with the scientific world-conception" (Hahn et al., 1929, 304–305).

In the last lines of the *Aufbau*'s preface, just after Carnap likened the Vienna Circle's pattern of collaborative work to that of the sciences, he ends:

> We feel that there is an inner kinship between the attitude on which our philosophical work is founded and the intellectual attitude which presently manifests itself in entirely different walks of life; we feel this orientation in artistic movements, especially in architecture, and in movements which strive for meaningful forms of personal and collective life, of education, and of external organization in general … Our work is carried by the faith that this attitude will win the future. (Carnap, 1928, xviii)

Aside from leadership of and participation in the Ernst Mach society, social and political engagement of members of the Vienna Circle also included a book series edited by Frank and Schlick, *Collected Works for the Scientific World-Conception* (Romizi, 2012). Neurath, Carnap, and Feigl held lectures in the Bauhaus, a prominent school of modernist architecture, arts, and design; Carnap's lecture was entitled "Science and Life" (Galison, 1990). The Bauhaus saw its own work as inherently political. This was also the time of *baupolitik* (politics through construction) in Vienna: the SDAP responded to immigration and mass homelessness in the wake of World War I with an ambitious public housing program. Neurath was centrally involved in the planning and execution of that program, working alongside modernist architects Adolf Loos and Josef Frank, brother of Vienna Circle member Philipp Frank (Cartwright et al., 1996).

Neurath also founded Vienna's Museum of Society and Economy, which focused on conveying central statistics about modern life to the working class, including the illiterate. To accomplish this, Neurath and his collaborators, Marie Reidemeister and Gerd Arntz, developed what came to be known as ISOTYPE (International System of Typographic Picture Education), thereby introducing modern-day pictographic signs well known not just for communicating statistical information but also pictographic communication in a variety of public-facing settings such as airports and train stations (Neurath and Kinross, 2009). Their goal of educating the working class was political, focused on ends such as contrasting the health of the wealthy with that of the working class and exposing falsehoods used to support racist ideas (Edmonds, 2020).

Home and Factory Weaving in England

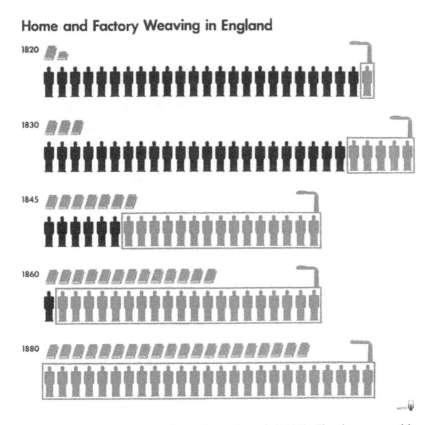

Figure 2 Example ISOTYPE figure from Neurath (1939). Simple, comparable-size objects are used to represent a fixed number of people or objects that can readily be compared to visually grasp statistical data. Each bolt of cloth represents 50 million pounds total production; each darker human figure (on the left) represents 10,000 home weavers; and each lighter human figure (enclosed within a factory shape) represents 10,000 factory weavers.

As suggested by what we've seen of the Vienna Circle's manifesto, several members of the Circle considered their philosophical work and their social and political activities to be connected. Neurath was a particularly salient example of this, as he was explicit and voluble about the connections in his writings, but Carnap, Hahn, Frank, and others also saw their philosophical research in relation to social and political projects. In 1930, Carnap and Hans Reichenbach, from the like-minded Berlin Society for Empirical Philosophy, took over leadership of a philosophy journal, renaming it *Erkenntnis* (*Knowledge*). In the editorial of its first issue, Reichenbach (1930) encouraged the submission of work oriented toward resolving social problems (see Cartieri and Potochnik, 2013).

2.3 From *Rotes Wien* to Mid-Century America

In the cultural context of the Vienna Circle, even philosophical work that to a contemporary eye seems thoroughly apolitical was politically valanced. Romizi (2012) argues that we should see the Vienna Circle's philosophical work as political not because it theorizes societal influence on science but rather insofar as its members were "politically engaged philosophers of science who chose to become institutionally visible and active as 'the Vienna Circle of the scientific world-conception'" (209). As I have touched on, the scientific conception of the world amounted to a political stance: this was intended as a contrast to *Weltanschauung* (worldview), which held particular significance in that political and social moment. Political parties that developed in Austria in the early twentieth century saw themselves as *Weltanschauungparteien*, each fighting to support a specific worldview (Romizi, 2012).

The Vienna Circle's rejection of metaphysics is perhaps the best known – and most often mocked –element of their philosophical stance. As Friedman (1996) discusses, the target of this rejection was the metaphysics that predominated in their milieu, namely, post-Kantian German idealism. Heidegger was one main target, as the embodiment of all that the Vienna Circle saw as problematic with this trend (e.g. Carnap, 1932). Neurath makes explicit what he took to be the political associations of this variety of metaphysics: "The idealistic philosophers of our day from Spann to Heidegger want to rule, as the theologians once ruled" (Neurath, 1932; quoted in Friedman, 1996, 51–52). Hahn and Carnap each criticized this brand of metaphysics as a way of distracting "the masses" from the need for social change, and Zilsel criticized the romanticization of genius (Edmonds, 2020). In opposition to this politically valanced metaphysics, the Vienna Circle, together with the Bauhaus and several other cultural movements of the time, embraced the *neue Sachlichkeit*, or new objectivity: a commitment to internationalism, socialism, and an anti-individualist and scientific orientation (Galison, 1990; Friedman, 1996).

Most members of the Vienna Circle had Jewish ancestry, at a time when this was a liability in Viennese society, as well as in pursuing a career at the University of Vienna. Regardless of whether and to what extent this might have influenced their intellectual work, it certainly influenced the reception of those contributions. Einstein's groundbreaking work in theoretical physics was viewed with hostility; a Working Group for German Scientists for the Preservation of Pure Science was founded to oppose relativity theory, deemed "Jewish physics," overly mathematical and lacking sufficient respect for the mystical. Fellow Viennese Otto Weininger wrote that "the spirit of modernity" itself was Jewish (Edmonds, 2020).

In 1934, Austria became a fascist, one-party state. Shortly after, the police disbanded the Ernst Mach Society on the grounds that it was aligned with the

SDAP, and police raided Neurath's office. Neurath was out of the country at the time, and Carnap sent word to him; he simply never returned to Vienna. Hahn died that year. Other members of the Vienna Circle began to lose their jobs and, over the next four years, almost all who were still alive emigrated. In 1936, Schlick, still in Vienna, was murdered by a former student. After Austria was unified with Hitler's Germany in 1938, Schlick's murderer was freed from jail on the grounds that the murder had been motivated by anti-Semitism.

The Vienna Circle's work in support of the scientific conception of the world was thus uprooted from its original cultural and political context, landing primarily in mid-century United States and Great Britain. Due to the changed cultural context as well as the changed political landscape after the end of World War II, the projects that continued had significantly changed associations. A prime example was Neurath's decades-long work toward unified science, including a conference series and ambitious book series, which he saw as deeply socialist but which was now criticized at length for its alleged fascism, first at the Fifth Congress for the Unity of Science and later in the pages of *Philosophy and Phenomenological Research* by Horace Kallen.

Reisch (2005) details how, in part due to this changed political landscape and in part due to accidental circumstances such as Neurath's early death, philosophy of science was transformed, pushed to "the icy slopes of logic." Reisch draws this phrase from the Vienna Circle's manifesto: "Of course not every single adherent of the scientific world-conception will be a fighter. Some, glad of solitude, will lead a withdrawn existence on the icy slopes of logic" (317). Transplanted into the political landscape of (for the most part) Cold War United States and Great Britain, members of the Vienna Circle who were less avowedly political, like Feigl, thrived, and some, like Carnap, became less politically active. Philosophy of science was transformed as a result: in its motivations, its primary focuses, and its intended audiences.

This transformation was visible in changes to the Philosophy of Science Association (PSA), the main professional association for philosophers of science in the United States, over the second half of the twentieth century. In 1948, the PSA bylaws specified that philosophy of science should include "the encouragement of practical consequences which may flow [from the study of philosophy of science] ... to men of good will in general ("Constitution and By-Laws of the Philosophy of Science Association," 1948, 176). Continuing into the 1950s, PSA members were encouraged to apply their views to social issues, but by the end of that decade, philosophy of science was withdrawing from social and political activity. The PSA mission narrowed considerably to "the furthering of studies and free discussion from diverse standpoints in the field of philosophy of science" and the language about practical benefits for all people had disappeared ("Revised

Constitution of the Philosophy of Science Association – 1958," 1959, 63; see Howard, 2003; Douglas, 2009). Interestingly, philosophy of science also seems to have grown in its separation from science at the same time. For example, the participation of philosophers of science in the annual conferences of the American Association for the Advancement of Science (AAAS) diminished (Douglas, 2009).

This transformation not only led philosophy of science to an apolitical orientation during the second half of the twentieth century; it also obscured the earlier political orientation. Some members of the Vienna Circle, and philosophical projects initiated by the Circle, continued to influence philosophy of science during this later period, and the new depoliticized version of the work was better known in anglophone philosophy than the original work. This obscured from view and ultimately from memory how the philosophical–scientific work of the Vienna Circle constituted a political stance in the cultural and political moment they occupied. From the perspective of contemporary philosophy of science, without attending to the political and cultural milieu and the scientific exchanges of the Vienna Circle, it is easy to misinterpret their work as narrowly focused on philosophical concerns in a purely academic context.

Yet it is worth unearthing this history to consider it as a model of the interrelationships among science, philosophy, and the public. Attending to this very different model reveals that how science and its philosophy relate to the public today is not inevitable. Philosophy and science can be, and have been, more closely related to each other and more directly engaged with public concerns and audiences. Moreover, this historic case study suggests that these interrelationships may be mutually supporting. Science and philosophy seeking public engagement may find more points of connection, and philosophy engaged more fully with science may in turn lead both to be more effective in their public engagement.

3 Public Understanding of Science

For seventy-five years, the Bulletin of the Atomic Scientists have run the Doomsday Clock, a metaphor for the risk of humanity's destruction. In 2023, the decision was made to move the clock to 90 seconds before midnight, intended to signify that if human history is a 24-hour day, human civilization is only 1.67 minutes from its end. This is the closest the clock has been to midnight in its seventy-five-year history. The indication of perilousness is due to risk of global nuclear war and the impending climate catastrophe.

Public understanding of the latter, anthropogenic climate change, is increasingly a focus of scientists, scientific institutions, and many more. One example is the Yale Program on Climate Change Communication, which researches "public climate change knowledge, attitudes, policy preferences, and behavior" and engages with the public about "climate change science and solutions."[5] Another example is the Climate Interpreters program of the National Network for Ocean and Climate Change Interpretation (NNOCCI), in which education staff at zoos, aquaria, museums, and more are trained in effective techniques to teach the public about climate change. There is no question that climate change significantly threatens security and well-being for many communities around the world. It is worth explicitly noting that improving public understanding of climate change science is taken to be a main step in addressing this threat.

More broadly, much of the attention on how the public relates to science is focused on public understanding of science. How effective is STEM education in elementary schools, high schools, and colleges? How well does the average person understand the state of scientific knowledge, and has this improved or worsened over time? This attention is borne out in regular updates to science curricular standards; in a variety of initiatives targeting informal science education in museums, zoos, and the like; and in attempts to assess public understanding of science. In the United States, the public has been regularly surveyed about its understanding of science since the 1950s; Great Britain began surveying the public on scientific literacy in 1988 (Miller, 2001). Since 2006, the Organisation for Economic Cooperation and Development (OECD) has administered tests of scientific literacy to fifteen-year-old students internationally every three years, with seventy-nine countries participating in 2018.

In this section, I focus on public understanding of science as one aspect of the public's relationship to science. This focus is also relevant to some of the obligations science bears to the public, as outlined in Section 1, including especially career pathways into STEM and public access to science's value, including knowledge and skills. In Section 3.1, I survey efforts to refine what is relevant to public understanding of science – from scientific facts to other focuses such as scientific methods and credibility – and explore how these different targets relate to how we define the goal of scientific literacy. Then, in Section 3.2, I investigate how philosophical research about the nature of scientific understanding may be relevant for public understanding of science as well – in particular, how achieving understanding requires developing the proper connection to those seeking understanding and how the objects of scientific understanding may vary according to the specific aim. Finally, in

---

[5] Yale Program on Climate Change Communication website: https://climatecommunication.yale .edu.

Section 3.3, I consider how identification and rejection of the "deficit model" of public understanding of science has shifted what is seen as relevant for promoting the aim of public understanding of science.

3.1 What Is the Goal of Understanding Science?

The OECD's international test of scientific literacy in high school students defines scientific literacy as consisting in three competencies:

- Explaining phenomena scientifically;
- Evaluating and designing scientific enquiry; and
- Interpreting data and evidence scientifically (OECD, 2019).

The first of these is intended to target content knowledge, while the second and third require knowledge of scientific methods and the rationale behind those methods. Together, these are taken to suffice for students to have the ability to assess scientific claims and media representations of those claims. These three competencies are a good characterization also of the focus of the survey questions the US National Science Foundation (NSF) has used for decades to gauge Americans' knowledge of scientific facts. That survey includes true/false questions about factual knowledge, such as "The center of the Earth is very hot"; a handful of questions about probability and experimental design; and one or a few questions about whether some pursuit (e.g. astrology) qualifies as scientific (Besley and Hill, 2020).

Scientific literacy thus seems to be broadly conceived as related to mastery of scientific content, scientific methods, and the rationale for those methods. Yet several questions remain about how the goal of public understanding of science should be conceived, including how scientific understanding should be assessed, what is important for the public to understand about science, and how scientific understanding can be effectively promoted. I introduce and motivate the first two questions in this section and address the third in Section 3.3. Of course, this brief discussion cannot hope to resolve these questions. The aim, instead, is merely to bring them into relief.

Turning first to the question of how scientific understanding is assessed, consider again the OECD's international test of scientific literacy and the NSF's long-standing survey of science literacy indicators, especially their focus on content knowledge and scientific methods. This focus is broadly shared by measures of scientific understanding, but it has also been the target of criticism. According to Pardo and Calvo (2004), "scientific literacy has been reduced to comprehension of central concepts and propositions about the natural world and some extremely stylized procedures or strategies for creating and validating knowledge" (205). These authors point out that, with respect to the true/false content knowledge questions used in the NSF survey and related British surveys, these questions chiefly target simple recall knowledge, their content does not reflect common science education standards, and there is no evidence that the small number of questions is a representative sample of content knowledge. They also point out that this approach tacitly assumes continuity of an individual's content knowledge across scientific fields rather than varying specialties. Stocklmayer and Bryant (2012) administered a science literacy survey to more than 500 scientists, who found the questions to be problematic and especially so for topics within their own discipline. Many could not recall the correct answers.

Resolving such questions about the reliability and validity of scientific literacy indicators is important for meaningful assessment of public understanding of science. There is work in psychometrics assessing these properties of scientific literacy surveys and developing improved instruments (e.g. Stocklmayer and Bryant, 2012; Kahan, 2017). Yet many evaluations of scientific literacy proceed without concern for this issue or, at least, set aside concerns and use the same survey instruments in order to permit historic comparisons (e.g. Besley and Hill, 2020). Assessments of reliability and validity also do not address the extent to which content knowledge and awareness of scientific methods are of central importance to public understanding of science and whether other facilities are more important.

This brings us to the second question raised earlier in the section, regarding what is important for the public to understand about science. Our brief consideration of how scientific literacy can be defined reveals that understanding of science might involve many distinct targets. Classically, these include grasping scientific knowledge about the world, or what we have termed content knowledge; important scientific methods, such as controlled experiments; and the rationale for or epistemic importance of these scientific methods. Other possible targets include grasping the social structure of science and its epistemic importance; societal roles played by scientific investigation and findings; and how to apply scientific findings or tools to one's own life.

Which of these targets is important, and to what extent, depends on the goal of public understanding of science. Is the goal to improve the everyday lives of individuals (Feinstein, 2011)? To facilitate broad and effective public use of scientific knowledge (Kahan, 2017)? To increase the ability of groups or individuals to make evidence-based decisions (Besley and Hill, 2020)? To improve the public's ability to know which scientific claims to believe and how to apply those claims (Keren, 2018)? To generate public support for the use of scientific research in solving societal problems (Chakravartty, 2022)? These goals differ in whether societal or individual capacities are at stake, and in whether they are practical, epistemic, or affective in nature. What practical, epistemic, or affective capacities for individuals and/or their support for societal capacities are supposed to be cultivated seems to matter very much to what it is the public is meant to understand about science.

Failure to distinguish among these various goals may reflect an assumption that simply better understanding science, that is, understanding things more like scientists do, is at once valuable for individuals' practical, epistemic, and affective capacities related to science and also for their support of science taking on appropriate societal roles. This kind of assumption often seems to lurk in the background of discussions of public understanding of science and the public's relationship to science more broadly, but it has been challenged.

Notice that which targets for scientific understanding promote which of these goals – or whether they promote any at all – is an empirical question. Feinstein (2011) criticizes a lack of attention to this question among those who study science literacy. He says:

> Our field has produced little evidence that any science taught in school, from Newton's laws to natural selection, helps people lead happier, more success-ful, or more politically savvy lives. There is an undeniable irony in this. Even researchers who dedicate their careers to promoting evidence-based educa-tional practices seem oddly content to accept broad and unsubstantiated claims about the usefulness of science in daily life. (169)

Feinstein (2011) argues that recent empirical investigations of scientific literacy have suggested three central features of public understanding of science: it is only meaningful if relevance is established to individuals' own lives; it is applicable not by lone individuals but within communities; and it is used within specific and varying community and cultural contexts. In his words, "people selectively integrate scientific ideas with other sources of meaning, connecting those ideas with their lived experience to draw conclusions and make decisions that are personally and socially meaningful" (180).

Based on these findings, Feinstein (2011) suggests that scientific literacy should be understood fundamentally as *engagement* with science, which is a relation that only outsiders can bear to the institution of science. Effective public understanding of science, on this view, consists not in helping the public to understand what scientists understand – turning the public into insiders to science – but rather in creating what Feinstein calls "competent outsiders." Competent outsiders to science know how to: (1) identify when science is relevant to their goals and (2) seek scientific expertise that furthers those goals. If Feinstein is right, it follows that identifying when and how science is relevant, for (1), and identifying and interpreting scientific expertise, for (2), are both fundamental to scientific literacy.

Keren (2018) also motivates a "competent outsider" conception of scientific literacy and discusses how different epistemic norms are relevant to competent outsiders. While reliance on the authority of experts and consensus views is not epistemically appropriate for scientists, these are important epistemic norms for scientifically literate outsiders. Keren also suggests that this reframing indicates how philosophy of science might be well positioned to contribute to public understanding of science. He points out that much philosophical work has focused on why, when, and about what to trust scientists and what qualifies as scientific consensus, both of which are, on this view, fundamental to scientific literacy. A related idea is that philosophy of science can be instrumental in teaching about scientific uncertainty and how scientific theories change over time, which is important to inoculating competent outsiders to science against cynical inculcation of doubt (see also Section 4).

In contrast to these approaches, Chakravartty (2022) emphasizes especially the goal of generating public support for effective societal use of scientific research. Prioritizing this goal leads Chakravartty to focus simply on the scientific literacy target of the instrumental success of science: that science is unrivaled in its ability to support effective action in the world. He characterizes science as "an extraordinary machine for generating our best hopes for responding to challenges inherent in our natural and social environments" (Chakravartty, 2022). This echoes the vision of science developed in Strevens's (2020) book for a broad audience, *The Knowledge Machine*, which features the same metaphor of science as a well-designed machine. Note that, in line with my broader point here, this priority for scientific literacy is yoked directly to the goal it supports. In particular, cultivating an appreciation for science's instrumental effectiveness can contribute to public support for scientific research and its societal use, but this does not in itself further the goal of individual or community access to and effective use of scientific knowledge.

In summary, there is not a single, obvious target for scientific literacy but a variety of potential targets: content knowledge, nature of epistemic warrant, abilities, identification of expertise, and appreciation of science's epistemic authority. Which are valuable and the extent of their value depends on the specific goals of scientific literacy. Improving individuals' everyday lives, deploying scientific knowledge effectively, the ability for evidence-based decision-making, and the ability to assess and apply scientific claims require different competencies and might be furthered by different targets for scientific literacy. Table 2 summarizes these potential goals and potential targets.

There is also a related question of the extent to which public understanding of science should mirror the capacities of practicing scientists. I introduced the

Table 2 Potential goals for scientific literacy and targets for scientific literacy. It cannot be presumed that each target for scientific literacy is equally valuable for achieving each goal; the value of each target must be assessed in relation to the goal(s) that are valued. (These are separate lists; the items in each row are not meant to be linked across columns.)

Potential goals of scientific literacy	Potential targets for scientific literacy
Improve everyday lives	Content of scientific knowledge
Facilitate broad and effective public use of scientific knowledge	Scientific methods and their rationale
	Ability to assess scientific claims
Increase the ability of groups or individuals to make evidence-based decisions	Identifying when science is relevant to one's goals
	How to seek scientific expertise that furthers one's goals
Improve the ability to know which scientific claims to believe and how to apply those claims	Identifying why, when, and about what to trust scientists
Engender public support for using scientific research to solve societal problems	That science supports effective action

view that the project of scientific literacy should be taken to be producing competent outsiders rather than scientists-in-training. One complication with this idea, though, is that it requires distinguishing whether someone will become an insider to science to inform how they should be taught about science. Yet, we have seen that a strikingly large percentage of people participate in STEM careers of one kind or another, and I will suggest in Section 5 that science may benefit from further expanding participation in science – professional and otherwise.

3.2 Scientific Understanding and Understanding Science

Philosophy of science has, of late, directed renewed attention to the topic of scientific understanding. Understanding has long been thought to be part and parcel of scientific explanation. For instance, Hempel (1965) specifies that "explanation enables us to *understand why* the phenomenon occurred" (337, emphasis in original). More recently, the nature of and requirements for scientific understanding have been investigated at a remove from discussions of scientific explanation, with a focus more on the subjective or cognitive features of achieving understanding. This has coincided with increased attention to understanding rather than knowledge in epistemology. Indeed, these discussions are partly overlapping and their contours similar, with some epistemology discussions arguing that understanding does not require knowledge and is thus not held to the same requirements of truth or objectivity.

In both philosophical contexts, some see attention to understanding as a way to focus additionally on the subjective, in the sense of the experience of the subjects of understanding or those who develop or possess scientific explanations. Philosophers who address understanding often invoke "grasping" as a term for the relation between subject and object of understanding. Some take this to be a mental ability that goes beyond mere belief, and thus that understanding goes beyond mere knowledge, whereas others think understanding is distinctive only in the nature of what is understood (see Grimm, 2021, for discussion).

In Potochnik (2017), I motivated this emphasis on the subjective aspects of understanding by noting that understanding has a dual nature: it is at once an epistemic achievement and a cognitive state. When one considers understanding as a cognitive state, it is clear that psychological characteristics are relevant to achieving this state. To understand, an epistemic subject must be in the proper cognitive relationship with the object of understanding, and the subject's psychological traits – both enduring and fleeting – are relevant to achieving that cognitive relationship. When one considers understanding as an epistemic achievement, it is also clear that understanding is subject to standards of success. A felt sense of understanding does not suffice for genuine understanding. Grimm (2012) stresses that "grasping" is a success term.

Even so, due to understanding's dual nature as an epistemic achievement and a cognitive state, success with the former – successfully grasping the object of understanding – depends also on the latter. In Potochnik (2017), I suggested this as the reason why departures from the truth to simplify or to otherwise make something more cognitively accessible can promote understanding. Several philosophers stress the value of idealizations to scientific understanding (e.g. de Regt, 2017; Elgin, 2017; Khalifa, 2017). Idealizations are simplifying false assumptions, such as the assumption that a planetary body is a point mass or the assumption that a population of organisms is infinite. Idealizations cannot straightforwardly contribute to accuracy or truth, as they are literally false. But they can directly facilitate understanding by supporting a subject's grasp of the object of understanding – by helping a subject achieve the cognitive state of understanding. (Presuming any such idealizations are consistent with the requirements for understanding as a legitimate epistemic achievement; what this requires is a matter of significant debate.)

The role of idealizations in facilitating understanding is a useful bridge from philosophical discussions of scientific understanding back to the topic of public understanding of science. One well appreciated role for idealizations in facilitating understanding is in the context of science textbooks; indeed, this is less controversial than the question of whether and to what extent idealizations can facilitate the understanding of scientists themselves, the typical target for discussions of scientific understanding. Simplifications, iterative discussion, and tracing the historical progression of ideas in a scientific field are all common strategies in textbooks to support student understanding.

I suggest that these topics – the nature of scientific understanding and what strategies support broad understanding of science – are more continuous than typically appreciated. For the former, attention has generally been directed at the relationship with the objects of understanding: what it is about the world that must be depicted and with what degree of accuracy to suffice for legitimate understanding. Strategies to render objects of understanding graspable to scientists have been relegated to the sidelines. For the latter, attention has generally been directed at the relationship with the subjects of understanding: what strategies can help public audiences grasp scientific findings. What about science should be understood and with what degree of accuracy has often not been adequately emphasized, as discussed in Section 1.1. Yet the questions are at root deeply similar. Cross-connections across investigations of these topics likely would improve both.

In my view, one important topic about scientific understanding has received insufficient attention in the literature on the nature of scientific understanding and also in the literature on public understanding of science. That topic is the extent to which the process of understanding and the nature of what is understood are both shaped by the specific features of what an audience seeks to understand.

In my view, specific priorities regarding what is to be understood shape the nature of the resulting understanding in significant ways. Scientists may say they aim to understand the western bluebird's colonization pattern, for example. But actual scientific research always targets a more specific question: how this colonization pattern relates to mountain bluebirds' dispersal, or how the pattern is influenced by variable testosterone levels in incubating eggs, or how the pattern is influenced by the introduction of a novel resource, and so on. As a result, scientific theories and models capture just a few of the features of the phenomena they aim to understand, ignoring or simplifying features that are incidental to present purposes. If one does not carefully attend to how scientific understanding is highly specific to limited goals, one risks seeing accounts that have distinct but related goals as in conflict with one another or seeing research questions as answered, phenomena as fully understood, when there are other questions that might still be asked. Scientists have regularly succumbed to both kinds of misimpressions (Potochnik, 2013).

This point has direct implications for public understanding of science. To begin with, understanding scientific findings might in part require understanding the specific aims those findings address. Further, it might be important to public understanding of scientific methods to appreciate how research is developed in response to specific aims, which can lead to multiple accounts of the same or closely related phenomena. Such a recognition is important insofar as multiple accounts of the same phenomena might otherwise be mistakenly thought to indicate scientists disagree about those phenomena – or even cynically employed by those wishing to inspire doubt about some socially controversial scientific research, like climate change or evolution.

This specificity of scientific research to its aims also provides a parallel to how the pursuit of public understanding of science itself depends on specific goals. As I described in Section 3.1, scientific literacy might be defined in any number of ways. Is it important for the general public to grasp: basic scientific facts, cutting-edge scientific discoveries, the methods responsible for science's success, why those methods lead to success, who should be trusted as a scientific expert, why those people should be trusted, and/or when science might be useful to one's own life and how to access relevant scientific findings and apply them in those instances? Each of these aims requires different approaches to promoting public understanding of science, just as different specific aims in science motivate different varieties of research.

3.3 How the Public Comes to Understand

This brings us to the third question introduced in Section 3.1, namely, how best to promote public understanding of science. Historically, the emphasis on content knowledge in assessments of scientific literacy was accompanied by what has been called the "deficit model" of public understanding of science. This is the view that public understanding of science is furthered by experts ameliorating a deficit in information or knowledge (Miller, 2001). On the deficit model, knowledge or information already possessed by experts suffices as the basis for better public understanding of science. This idea is suggested, for instance, by Kahan's (2017) brief characterization of the project of public understanding of science as "how ordinary citizens come to know what is collectively known by science" (1013).

The deficit model is now widely criticized as inadequate. One problem is the implication of one-way communication. This problem is addressed by moving to a communication framework of two-way dialogue or mutual exchange (Miller, 2001). Just as understanding is shaped by its aims, it is also shaped by the constellation of beliefs, values, and concerns it is met with, for – recall – understanding is both an epistemic achievement and a cognitive state. This broader constellation of cognitive and affective states is always relevant to one's understanding of a given topic, including about science, and may well shape the exchange.

A second problem with the deficit model is the assumption that the communication of facts is all that is needed to increase understanding. This problem is addressed, at least in part, by taking seriously the components of scientific literacy discussed in Section 3.1, namely, viewing public understanding of science to consist in abilities relevant to individuals' contexts: the ability to identify when science is relevant to their goals and the ability to seek scientific expertise that furthers those goals. Scientists do not have all these answers. Criticisms of the deficit model have also inspired a move away from the focus of public understanding of science to other focuses instead, such as public trust in science, but I save that topic for Section 4.

Rejection of a deficit-model approach to public understanding of science is also sometimes accompanied by an interest in how sociology, history, and philosophy of science can support the project of public understanding of science (e.g. Miller, 2001). These disciplines can, as noted, provide insight variously into the nature and limits of scientific expertise; the position(s) that science occupies in society; and how scientific knowledge, practices, and social positions have changed over time. Potochnik et al. (2018) is one recent attempt to provide a philosophically rich discussion of these topics at an undergraduate level.

Moving away from a deficit-model approach to public understanding of science should not be taken to suggest that all parties to an exchange are equally expert in all matters. As Miller (2001) points out, "Scientists and lay people are not on the same footing where scientific information is concerned, and knowledge, hard won by hours of research, and tried and tested over the years and decades, deserves respect" (118). Instead, conceiving of the project of public understanding of science as dialogue and knowledge generation, rather than one-way knowledge transfer, takes seriously the specialization of expertise in contemporary society. We can expect that all parties to public exchanges about science have different kinds of relevant expertise to bring to the table. The goal of such exchanges is thus to co-create new, contextually situated knowledge about science and its particular, contextual relevance.

This reframing of the project of public understanding of science stems from prioritizing the value of people's ability to identify when science is relevant to their goals and to seek scientific expertise that furthers those goals. As Feinstein (2011) puts the point, "the pursuit of science literacy is not *incidentally* but *fundamentally* about identifying relevance: learning to see how science is or could be significant to the things you care about most" (180, emphasis in original). This aim for scientific literacy changes the relevance of public understanding of basic scientific facts and cutting-edge scientific discoveries. Understanding these is not so much an aim of scientific literacy as, at most, a means. Here is Miller (2001):

> Communicators might also consider that factual communications – while they may be inspirational – probably have little lasting effect on knowledge levels. People will pick up the knowledge they need for the task at hand, use it as required, and then put it down again. It will not be ready to hand when the survey interviewer next asks them if, for example, an electron is bigger than an atom. (118)

In light of criticisms of recall-focused assessments of scientific literacy reviewed in Section 3.1, it seems this is so not only for the nonspecialist public but for scientists as well (Stocklmayer and Bryant, 2012). For scientists and nonscientist members of the public alike, literacy amounts not to mastery of a broad, stable body of knowledge but rather to knowing how to situationally apply abilities to achieve targeted understanding.

4 Public Trust in Science

The NSF's long-standing survey of science literacy indicators was introduced in Section 3. The short list of questions about "basic scientific facts" has remained unchanged over decades, to enable longitudinal study. But two of those questions are no longer included in the data about trends in scientific literacy. These two questions concern the Big Bang and human evolution, two culturally divisive topics of scientific investigation. The original NSF science literacy survey asks whether the following claims are true: "Human beings, as we know them today, developed from earlier species of animals" and "The universe began with a big explosion." The percentage of respondents that mark each as true (the correct answer) lags the percentage who respond correctly to the other scientific fact questions.

In 2018, survey respondents were randomly given either these original questions or alternative questions (changes italicized): "*Elephants*, as we know them today, developed from earlier species of animals" and "*According to astronomers*, the universe began with a huge explosion." The evolution alternative question changes the focus away from the hot-button topic of human evolution but is identical in its relation to evolutionary theory. The Big Bang alternative question changes the question from what is true to *what scientists think* is true. With these changes, correct responses increased from 49 percent to 68 percent for evolution, and from 38 percent to 65 percent for the Big Bang (Besley and Hill, 2020).

This demonstrates that there is more that contributes to participants' responses to these questions than scientific literacy alone. This is hardly a surprise; the origins of human life and of the universe are topics with deep relationships to religious identity and worldviews. Whether one answers in accordance with scientific theory has less to do with scientific literacy and more to do with one's personal and social identity. Indeed, Kahan (2017) finds that higher scores on his revised test of scientific literacy is associated with increased political polarization on evolution, the Big Bang, and also climate change. That is, for individuals with conservative political views, increased scientific literacy actually *decreases* the likelihood of responding in agreement with scientific consensus on these three topics.

As this illustrates, understanding is not the only relevant relation between the public and science, and increasing public understanding of science does not inevitably lead to greater acceptance of and support for science. Public opinion of science and the public's tendency to accept claims and make decisions based on scientific findings are also shaped by personal and social identity, including religious views, political affiliation, and more. Knowing what ideas scientists endorse is not enough to guarantee accepting those ideas oneself. The gap between these must be filled with trust that the scientists are right on these matters. This move from a focus on public understanding of science to public trust in science is sometimes associated with a rejection of the deficit model introduced in Section 3.

Public trust in science – that is, the public believing and acting in accordance with scientific consensus – can have practical importance, as with willingness to participate in vaccination campaigns and prioritizing climate change mitigation. Public trust in science is also crucial for individuals and institutions to share in the epistemic goods science generates – part of science's obligation to the public outlined in Section 1 – and, ultimately, for science to maintain its social position. This section focuses on public trust in science. In Section 4.1, I consider how science denial has been conceived and targeted for intervention and discuss some recent philosophical accounts of why science is worthy of trust. Section 4.2 engages with the crucial and vexing question of evaluating scientific expertise, which is one key ingredient of public trust in science. Finally, in Section 4.3, I examine whether we are in the throes of a crisis in public trust in science and – to the extent that this is accurate – both how public distrust may be ameliorated and also how science can be more deserving of trust.

4.1 Science Denial

In Section 3, we discussed the ability to determine why, when, and about what to trust scientists as a potentially important target for scientific literacy. "Science denial" is a common term for the absence of this ability and, in particular, for the rejection of scientific consensus as a basis for trusting a finding or recommendation. Science denial has received extensive popular and academic attention in recent years, as hot-button social issues with significant implications, like uptake of the Covid-19 vaccine and willingness to prioritize climate change mitigation, are viewed by some as decided by scientific evidence and viewed by others as grounds for questioning scientific consensus on these topics and sometimes even science's worth in general.

McIntyre (2021) identifies five features of science denial supported by empirical research into the phenomenon. These include, first, cherry-picking evidence to support doubt of some scientific conclusion; second, belief in highly speculative theories that cannot be tested against evidence; and third, using flawed reasoning to maintain one's favored conclusion. These three features all relate to a failure to attend properly to scientific evidence. A fourth feature relates to scientific expertise: electing to trust the expertise of outsiders challenging near consensus in science rather than the near consensus. Fifth, science denial often involves criticizing scientific research for failing to meet standards of perfection: 100 percent expert agreement, complete certainty, or fully exhaustive evidence. These five features are hallmarks of motivated reasoning to dispute scientific findings held to be unacceptable for one reason or another.

Bardon (2020) surveys how science denial can arise out of self-serving motivations, as well as a variety of other common psychological tendencies, including in-group thinking, identity-protective cultural cognition, and even personality. Shifting the focus from what the public understands about scientific knowledge to whether and in what regards the public – and what segments of the public – trusts science as a source of knowledge brings attention squarely to human psychological tendencies. And the question is generally not about whether to trust at all, but rather about whom to trust, a decision that is shaped by social identity. As Bardon (2020) puts the point, "Identity informs the perception of expertise" (102).

In the present-day United States, relevant identity considerations for one's trust in science include at least in part political identity. Bardon surveys work revealing a decline in trust of science among political conservatives in the United States from 1974 to 2010. The perception that trust in science is politically polarized is illustrated by the widespread yard signs posted by political liberals featuring some variation of the following: "In this house, we believe: Black lives matter; Women's rights are human rights; No human is illegal; Science is real; Love is love; Kindness is everything." Such signs explicitly include trust in science on a list of values-based commitments commonly associated with liberal ideology.

The intersection between public trust in science and social identity is important for understanding and intervening on public trust in science – and, indirectly, on public understanding of science – insofar as different identity groups respond in different ways to scientific messaging (Bardon, 2020, 113). Bardon (2020) surveys research by McCright et al. (2013) suggesting that political conservatives report less trust in science with environmental and public health impacts, while political liberals report less trust in science with economic impacts via new innovations. Researchers have investigated how different approaches to climate change messaging vary in their effectiveness across political identities, nationalities, and more. For instance, Gustafson et al. (2020) found that US conservatives' support for renewable energy was driven more by considerations of economic impact, while US liberals' support was driven more by concern about climate change.

Attempts to ameliorate science denial rest on an implicit premise that science is trustworthy, such that its findings should not be denied but accepted. This has been a primary target of philosophical investigation: What features of science are responsible for its epistemic value? As Naomi Oreskes (2019) puts the question in her book's title, "Why Trust Science?"

Oreskes addresses this question with a walk through the history of science. She outlines an old idea about the source of science's trustworthiness, which she traces back to Comte, that the scientific method offers verification through empirical evidence. But, Oreskes suggests, philosophy, history, and sociology of science have since determined that there is not a singular scientific method and that scientific findings might well be jettisoned later. Oreskes's alternative answer to why we should trust science is: "(1) its sustained engagement with the world and (2) its social character" (Oreskes, 2019, 55). She acknowledges that this has not always sufficed to produce trustworthy science: conflicts of interest, racism and sexism, and insufficient diversity or dissent in a scientific community have all led to scientific findings that, in retrospect, were untrustworthy. Nonetheless, this is the source of science's general trustworthiness and what we can target for improving science's trustworthiness when doing so is necessary.

Michael Strevens (2020) also responds to this question of the basis for science's epistemic expertise. His account emphasizes how science's effectiveness depends upon the epistemic norm of limiting relevant considerations to empirical evidence alone. The drive for empirical evidence inspires scientists to go to great lengths to generate experimental or observational successes. This is similar to Oreskes's focus on science's sustained engagement with the world, but Strevens emphasizes how this engagement excludes other considerations. This feature of ultimate reliance on empirical evidence (and empirical evidence alone) is often emphasized as a sense in which science is objective. Elliott (2022) describes how the aim of public trust in science has been used to motivate science's freedom from the influence of values, as Liam Kofi Bright (2018) emphasizes in the work of Du Bois. Although many philosophers have challenged the idea that science is free from values, this ultimate reliance on empirical evidence – and the pursuit of additional empirical evidence – at least provides basic limitations on the extent of the influence of values on scientific findings.

Yet it is well established that sheer intellectual capacity, level of education, and increased factual knowledge do not protect against science denial. We have also seen that there is a disconnect between scientific literacy and trust in science. Science's trustworthiness seems to rely on more than just its epistemic authority. Goldenberg (2023) suggests that the additional ingredient needed regards motivation. She suggests that science expertise is trustworthy when it combines epistemic competence, moral reliability, and working in the public interest. A difficulty with working in the public interest as a requirement for science's trustworthiness is that scientists and the institutions of science do not always – and historically have not always - met this requirement. It thus may be that we cannot provide a general account of why all science is trustworthy – insofar as not all science is trustworthy.

A different strategy to address science denial suggests doing so in targeted ways. McIntyre (2021) acknowledges a role for widespread public understanding of the nature of science's epistemic authority in counteracting science denial, but he also urges scientists and others to directly address denial where it crops up. McIntyre has in mind a cadre of people who can directly engage with others in their orbit who endorse one or another belief that contradicts scientific knowledge, such as climate change denial or vaccine refusal. The tools he suggests, based on others' research, include personal engagement on an individual level when trust has been cultivated, emphasizing the existence of scientific consensus, using charts and graphs to render a problem tangible, and directly challenging the substance of the science denial or the reasoning being used to support it.

Bardon's (2020) proposed approach, also inspired by others' research, focuses not on broad public understanding of science's epistemic authority or combating existing science denial so much as achieving consensus and shared action in the face of continued polarization. He suggests, first, communicating in ways that are less likely to threaten social identity or heighten defensive protection of one's beliefs and, second, emphasizing local concerns and shared identities. On the first point, the suggestion is that science communication should employ message framing that counteracts or even makes use of any motivated reasoning at play. Messaging can appeal to values held by those resistant to the scientific knowledge at issue rather than threatening those values. Climate-change messaging to a politically conservative audience, for instance, might emphasize the economic benefits of renewable energy (Gustafson et al., 2020). The second point, emphasizing local and small-group intervention, suggests the importance of trusted messengers, perhaps that share the social identities under threat. This is also an emphasis in Goldenberg (2021), who advocates for the importance of primary care practitioners in achieving vaccine uptake.

Our communities will always include people with a variety of religious and political identities, different constellations of concerns, and varying degrees of enthusiasm for science. The goal should not be to force those who reject scientific knowledge of one sort or another to change their social identities, values, and personal proclivities. Rather, the goal is to demonstrate how action based on scientific knowledge – climate change mitigation, vaccination, public health policies – is consistent with a variety of identities, values, and proclivities, even as these identities, values, and proclivities may remain of more central personal importance than scientific knowledge. Halpern and Elliott (2022) advocate for science communication to be thought of as "opportunities for meaning making around shared experiences" (621). Attempts to convert science denial to science acceptance must keep this goal of rendering science-based action consistent with a range of identities and values at the forefront in order to avoid merely playing into the existing cultural and political polarization. Consciously employing message framing to counteract motivated reasoning need not be a cynical maneuver to exploit those targeted but rather an opportunity to rethink one's own implicit assumptions about the social identities and values relevant to scientific research.

4.2 Evaluating Scientific Expertise

As we have seen, the project of cultivating scientific trust consists at least in part in creating the conditions for scientific expertise to guide people's decisions (when this expertise is relevant). This was also suggested as a potential target for scientific understanding in Section 3. This might at first sound simple: we should all trust scientists about matters of scientific knowledge. Indeed, the discussion in Section 3 about educating the public in how to seek scientific expertise presumes a simple target: a single source of relevant scientific expertise that is fully trustworthy and known to be so. In contrast to this simple picture, establishing the nature of scientific expertise relevant to a matter of public concern is often not easy.

First, on many topics, there is a variety of potentially relevant sources of scientific expertise. There's not usually a single, uniform scientific consensus issuing a decisive judgment on matters of public concern. One reason for this is the essential openness of science to revision. Disagreement, even on foundational issues, can be important. Another reason is the idea introduced in Section 3 that different scientific accounts capture just a few of the features of the phenomena they aim to understand, ignoring or simplifying other features, giving rise to multiple accounts that respond to different specific goals. It is not a simple matter to wade through the variety of potentially relevant scientific findings to fish out those that are most relevant.

Second, scientific expertise should not be considered decisive and impervious to criticism. As Goldenberg (2021) puts the point, "Contemporary scientific experts, while still afforded respect and considerable recognition, do not stand above public scrutiny and opinion; nor should they" (152). Inmaculada de Melo-Martín and Kristen Intemann (2018) stress that dissent is crucial for science to function effectively. Indeed, this is bound up in Oreskes's (2019) emphasis on the importance of science's social character and in feminist philosophy of science research supporting the crucial contribution of social structure to securing objectivity (e.g. Longino, 1990, 2002; Harding, 1991). Science denial is simply dissent that we judge to be inappropriate or unwarranted. Yet de Melo-Martín and Intemann (2018) offer compelling reasons to doubt our ability to distinguish problematic denial from warranted dissent based on the motives of those urging dissent, violation of the norms of science, or inappropriate assumption of risk. It is no simple matter to sort warranted dissent from science denial.

The evaluation of scientific expertise is thus bound up with the project of public trust in science and, indeed, must be resolved for science denial to even be diagnosed. To illustrate the challenge and how it has sometimes played out, Goldenberg (2021) develops and explores the trope of *the maverick* – a "scientific antihero" who is freethinking and unorthodox, standing up against the weight of establishment science. She offers Andrew Wakefield as an illustration of the type, infamous from his efforts to link the childhood MMR (measles, mumps, and rubella) vaccine to autism. Although the research findings have been thoroughly debunked, Wakefield's public advocacy campaign has been incredibly effective, with disastrous impacts on public health. Goldenberg emphasizes that any distrust, warranted or not, of the scientific establishment fuels support for the maverick. Her maverick trope shows how problematic individuals can benefit from distrust in the scientific establishment while still inheriting some of the broad implicit trust in science.

One common attempt to solve the problem of evaluating scientific expertise relies on scientific consensus. Oreskes (2019), for example, emphasizes that it is only scientific consensus that is worthy of public trust. But, as Goldenberg's maverick trope illustrates, it is not always a simple matter to identify when such a consensus exists. Consensus cannot require 100 percent agreement among scientists in relevant areas; this is too high a standard. There will always be mavericks in science, legitimate and otherwise, who do not agree with the consensus view. But when there is anywhere short of complete agreement among scientists in relevant areas, a metric is needed to judge whether a majority agreement qualifies as consensus. De Melo-Martín and Intemann (2018) also compellingly argue that no general technique of emphasizing scientific consensus in the face of dissent effectively targets just science denial and not warranted dissent. They consider the possibility of distinguishing between these with reference to the intent behind the dissent, the approach taken in the dissent, and the riskiness of the dissent, and find each fails to differentiate problematic from warranted dissent. So, the issue of evaluating scientific expertise cannot be solved by appeal to scientific consensus. Outlying disagreement is all but inevitable, and, as Oreskes's earlier work has famously demonstrated, cynical actors can be quick to use any disagreement within science to signal a reason for doubt (Oreskes and Conway, 2011).

Appealing to scientific consensus thus does not provide a shortcut around evaluating scientific expertise. It seems the public needs to be in the position to evaluate scientific expertise for themselves. This suggests the ability to evaluate scientific expertise might be one goal for scientific literacy. Anderson (2011) suggests that public evaluation of scientific expertise is obtainable. She argues that this evaluation should include identification of whether there is consensus among experts, and evaluation of whether a given individual qualifies as a trustworthy expert. Anderson argues that such an evaluation is widely available to nonexperts, though it is also undermined by current challenges in media and information flow. Goldenberg (2021) uses her trope of the maverick to illustrate how public evaluation of scientific expertise can be undermined by distrust of the traditional markers of professional scientific expertise and of in-group membership. To the extent that public trust in science is at issue, the groundwork is not in place to evaluate scientific expertise with reference to the social structure of science, as the latter has been deemed suspect.

There is surely a project of scientific literacy consisting in better educating the public regarding when and how to seek scientific expertise. But what this discussion reveals is that such instruction requires an existing foundation of trust in science. To the extent that the public – or specific communities – has real or imagined grounds for distrusting the scientific enterprise in its entirety, evaluation of scientific expertise cannot be used as a way out of that distrust.

4.3 A Crisis of Trust

Is there a new problem of trust in science, a crisis in trust? According to Oreskes (2019), there is: "The idea that science should be our dominant source of authority about empirical matters – about matters of fact – is one that has prevailed in Western countries since the Enlightenment, but it can no longer be sustained without an argument" (18).

This statement accords with broad observations of a "post-truth" era, where feelings and snap judgments matter more than established facts. (Oxford dictionaries named "post-truth" word of the year in 2016.) On the other hand, Bardon (2020) points out how, despite decline in support for science among political conservatives in the United States, science remains relatively popular, with 76 percent of the US public trusting scientists to act in the public interest, which is higher than the verdict regarding politicians, the media, or religious leaders.

It is apparent that there are novel challenges, or challenges at a novel scale, facing public trust in science. The Internet and social media have expanded communicative reach and flattened traditional hierarchies of information flow (O'Connor and Weatherall, 2019). Traditional media and new media alike increasingly cater to specific segments of the public, with a growing number of news sources providing coverage tailored to the views of some segment. We have also witnessed the cynical manipulation of public opinion against science for political reasons (Oreskes and Conway, 2011). Today's needs of supporting trust in science and addressing distrust are shaped by all of these challenges, and approaches to managing science denial must address these challenges. For example, van der Linden et al. (2017) have advocated "prebunking" rather than denial debunking – inoculating public audiences against future cynical efforts to induce science denial. And internet resources supporting evaluation of scientific expertise are increasingly common.

As this illustrates, new challenges have shifted the needs for public understanding of science. These perhaps also put additional pressure on the question of whether scientific literacy is central to how members of the public relate to science. Recall from Section 3 that rejections of the deficit model of public understanding of science have inspired focus on other relationships besides understanding. One example of this, as Bardon (2020) points out, is recent research suggesting that scientific curiosity may be more facilitative of openness to changing views on polarized issues than is scientific literacy. Cultivating awe and interest, helping people see science as something that can interest them, might be just as important as improved scientific literacy (Halpern and Elliott, 2022).

Goldenberg (2021) describes how the same instances of mistrust of science – her focus is vaccine hesitancy – can be framed either as a war on scientific expertise or as a crisis of trust. The "war on science" framing emphasizes the role of the science denier and the need to intervene on the denial, whereas the "crisis of trust" framing emphasizes the need for science to be trustworthy and its trustworthiness to be effectively communicated. Goldenberg (2021) suggests that the focus on science denial is itself an aspect of the war on science framing. With a focus on science denial, the need to increase public trust in science is understood as a need to influence the untrusting public, rather than a need to improve the trustworthiness of the institutions of science. The war on science framing mourns the death of expertise, but Goldenberg points out that expertise is alive and well: the question is simply where it is sought: "In a reinforcing cycle, people pursue unconventional sources of health information because they are not satisfied with official expert communications" (139). Goldenberg argues that it is more productive to adopt the framing of a crisis of trust instead of a war on science. This alternative framing "calls on scientific experts to be part of an active bridging response rather than lament the end of expertise" (169). Goldenberg urges scientific experts and institutions to respond to institutional shortcomings, including discrimination and improper influence from industry, so as to be more deserving of public trust, and to appeal to shared values and priorities in communication with public stakeholders.

De Melo-Martín and Intemann (2018) come to similar conclusions. As we have seen, they argue for the inability to decisively distinguish inappropriate attempts to sow dissent from warranted criticism of science. One of the concluding messages of their book is that it is valuable to investigate how trust in science can be cultivated, as well as how science can be worthier of trust. They say, "When institutional and social practices facilitate and sustain warranted public trust, people will be more likely to find consensus views credible" (150). Not clear consensus alone, but also transparency in the basis for conclusions and addressing conflicts of interest, scientific misconduct, improper influence of values, and science reaching beyond its domain of expertise into policy all help support greater public trust in scientific conclusions.

Goldenberg (2021) and de Melo-Martín and Intemann (2018) point to a special problem of mistrust of science in marginalized communities. In some marginalized communities, such as Black and Hispanic and Latino communities, there is warranted mistrust of science, especially medicine, due to a long history of unjust medical practices and medical research unresponsive to their communities' needs. This is not misplaced distrust that can be remedied by more clearly describing the nature of science's epistemic authority. Rather, it is warranted distrust that requires new solutions. I will circle back to the topic of warranted distrust of science at the end of Section 5.

According to Oreskes (2019), the goal for public trust in science is "informed trust in the consensual conclusions of scientific communities" (60). On Goldenberg's (2021) gloss, the goal is "well-placed trust in expert sources" (164). Trust inherently involves choosing to accept another's authority. But the requirement of "informed" or "well-placed" trust indicates that scientific institutions must earn and maintain the trust of the public. The acceptance of misinformation instead of scientific knowledge is a downstream symptom of a crisis in trust. The most direct influence the institutions of science have over this crisis in trust is with regard to their own practices, which are instrumental to the trustworthiness of science. Improvements to these practices might include expanding diversity and equity in science; addressing financial conflicts of interest and industry influence, especially on health research; addressing the improper influence of values; transparently communicating the basis for scientific conclusions; and targeting scientific and public health messaging to address communities' values and concerns (de Melo-Martín and Intemann, 2018; Goldenberg, 2021).

Thus, expanding public trust in science is not just an exercise in educating the public about the content of scientific knowledge and the nature of scientific expertise. What is needed is a public with (1) warranted belief that the institution of science is trustworthy and (2) the ability to sift through a variety of potentially relevant scientific sources of expertise, knowing when to defer to scientific expertise and when (and how) to attend to challenges from mavericks and outsiders. Notice that this might inform our selection among the goals for scientific literacy identified in Section 3. The epistemic authority of science is undoubtedly great, but a sober look at the scientific establishment also reveals ways in which science could be made more deserving of the trust of all segments of the public.

5 Participation in Science

Behind any scientific investigation are people: scientists, their postdocs, students, and lab techs – also their employers, their funders, the colleagues who will read their articles, the journalists they may or may not correspond with about their research. All of these people have cultural backgrounds, are members of social communities, and have their own personal takes on things. Any examination of science and the public would be incomplete without considering the people – members of the public in their own right – that conduct, support, and communicate science. This section thus focuses on participation in science.

This focus is also inspired by the end point of the previous chapter: the need for science as an institution to improve its trustworthiness is an important facet of science's general obligation to the public that I sketched in Section 1. Perhaps part of the solution is to expand participation in science, especially from communities and other groups typically underrepresented in and underserved by science.

Expanded participation in science can take two forms. First, this can involve a larger number or wider range of people becoming professionally engaged in scientific research, which relates to the widely recognized priority of increased diversity of STEM practitioners. Second, this can involve the participation of amateurs in scientific research, which is a research tradition in a variety of natural and social sciences, ranging from astrophysics to community psychology. I discuss each of these forms of participation in turn, the first in Section 5.1 and the second in Section 5.2, considering the significance of each for science's relationship to public institutions and communities. In Section 5.3, I consider the promise of expanded participation in science to improve science's trustworthiness and, more broadly, public trust in science.

5.1 Diversity and Agendas

One obvious way to expand participation in science is to increase the variety of types of people who pursue STEM careers. Conceived most broadly, diverse participation in science means that the professional participants in science (researchers, graduate students, laboratory technicians, and more) embody a wide variety of traits. Swartz et al. (2019) list the traits relevant to diversity in science as including: "background, age, gender, sexual orientation, race, ethnicity, culture, religion, geography, disability, socioeconomic status, area of expertise, level of experience, thinking style, and skill set" (S33). Often, special attention is placed on traits that relate to social identity, and especially social identities underrepresented in science. This is because underrepresentation of some social identity or identities results in the institution of science varying systematically from the surrounding society. Social identities underrepresented in contemporary science include (at least) women, sexual and gender minorities, racial and ethnic minorities, residents of the Global South, people with disabilities, first-generation college students, and people from low socioeconomic backgrounds. Special attention is also generally placed on the diversity of lead researchers: academic and nonacademic scientists, engineers, and medical researchers and professionals. These positions tend to be more visible and better compensated than other careers in STEM, and the people in these positions collectively tend to be less diverse, with a number of social identities significantly underrepresented in comparison to the broader population.

There is now a great deal of attention to improving diversity, equity, and inclusion in STEM education and STEM careers – that is, to increasing the extent to which the range of social identities of professional participants in science mirrors the range of identities in society at large. In the United States, the NSF has long prioritized broadening the participation of groups underrepresented in STEM – including women, minorities, and people with disabilities – in its funding opportunities and its strategic plans. Diversity, equity, and inclusion is also a focus area of the AAAS, which conceives of its role as to "expand access to STEM education, strengthen and diversify the science and technology workforce, and amplify underrepresented and marginalized voices within STEM."[6]

In philosophy, the value of diversified professional participation in science has been discussed in depth in literatures on feminist philosophy of science and on relationships between values and science. Those discussions have largely focused on the epistemic grounds for diversified professional participation. These are of central importance, but I want to consider first how ethical considerations motivate diversifying professional participation in science. Earlier discussion in this Element immediately suggests one ethical motivation, namely, greater equity and inclusion. Professional participation in science is a very important interface between science and the public. As mentioned in Section 1, 23 percent of the total US workforce in 2019 participated in STEM careers (Okrent and Burke, 2021). Professional participation in science provides direct benefit in the form of monetary compensation and social status, and it may also provide indirect benefits such as an insider status in science and epistemic advantage related to increased scientific literacy.

Professional participation in science should be as inclusive as possible for reasons of justice. This is especially crucial insofar as a number of social groups have historically been excluded from and underserved by science. Recall the discussion of science's obligation to society in Section 1. There, I suggested that, due to science's contribution to social inequality, the institution of science bears an obligation to ameliorate inequalities; creating and expanding support for diversified professional participation in science is one obvious way to respond to that obligation. Further, I suggested that extensive societal investment in science education has created an obligation for the institution of science to recompense this with career pathways, opportunities to participate professionally in science. Such opportunities should be afforded maximum equitability. Both of these obligations are meaningfully advanced by the institutions of science putting resources toward expanding diverse participation in science.

A second reason for diversifying professional participation in science concerns the benefit this has simply for the sheer number of people pursuing STEM careers. To the extent that people with social identities underrepresented in science have less ready access to educational opportunities and career advancement in science, this artificially depresses the number of people with pathways into STEM careers. This reason for greater diversity in science is implicit in the "pipeline" metaphor that was, at least until recently, predominant in discussions of equitable science education and career pathways. The motivation behind this

---

[6] AAAS website: www.aaas.org/diversity-equity-inclusion.

argument is ultimately epistemic: scientific knowledge is advanced faster and more fully the more able minds are recruited to participate in its advancement. As Goldenberg (2021) puts the point: "when scientific training is accessible and inclusive for traditionally underrepresented groups, the most talented workforce can be generated" (179).

A third reason for increased diversity in science, also epistemic in its motivation, stems from the recognition that not just sheer numbers of scientists but also the inclusion of scientists with different perspectives and values contributes to knowledge production. In this case, the advantage lies in making available different starting points that may prove fruitful, as well as opening up additional angles for critique. Ideas cultivated in feminist theory and feminist philosophy of science have been used to motivate this idea, including standpoint epistemology (Harding, 1991) and contextual empiricism (Longino, 1990, 2002). Over time, this reason to prioritize diversity in science has gained wide traction in academic science and in popular media. This benefit of expanded diversity in science does not simply motivate greater diversity within existing scientific institutions, as these are disproportionately Western and incorporate Western priorities and methods, but also motivates greater international diversity in scientific institutions (Sanches de Oliveira and Baggs, 2023).

These last two reasons to invest in a diversified STEM workforce concern science's intrinsic aims of knowledge production, while the first reason I mentioned, a basic consideration for equity of access, is about science's relationship to the public. A fourth reason for diversity in science brings us back to consideration of science's relationship to the public: a greater diversity of professional scientists is an opportunity for more communities to have direct personal connections with scientists and to see their values and priorities reflected in the practitioners of science. This is relevant to science's relationship to the public insofar as expansive personal connections into science can be expected to expand public support for science, to assist with scientific literacy – especially in identifying relevant scientific expertise – and thereby to increase the perception of science's trustworthiness. This connects to the facet of science's obligation to society outlined in Section 1 that consists in cultivating the trustworthiness of science.

These reasons for diversified professional participation in science are summarized in Table 3, which also includes one further reason I motivate just below. One rationale for cataloguing these many reasons is that each stems from different motivations, and each leads to somewhat different goals for the diversification of science. Of course, one need not choose among these reasons, as all can be furthered by broad attention to diversifying professional participation in science. But this does highlight different types of motivations and different prioritizations that efforts to diversify science might have.

Table 3 Reasons to diversify professional participation in science, and their goals and motivations.

Reason to diversify professional participation	Motivation for reason	Goal of diversification
Justice and equity of participation	Ethical: science's obligation to ameliorate inequality and distribute career pathways	Equitable sharing in the benefits of professional participation in science
Additional scientific talent	Epistemic: increasing the successful development of scientific knowledge	Maximizing involvement of prospective professional scientists
Diversifying perspectives and values	Epistemic: increasing the successful development of scientific knowledge	Maximizing breadth of perspectives and values shaping research
Expanding science's relationship to the public	Practical and ethical: support for science; science's obligation to cultivate trustworthiness	Maximizing breadth of social connections with professional scientists
Enhancing the epistemic accountability of science	Political: science's obligation to generate knowledge and products in society's best interests	Maximizing the extent to which scientific knowledge serves public and community priorities

I will develop in a bit more depth one further reason to diversify professional participation in science, namely, ensuring that scientific advances reflect public priorities, and the priorities of a greater range of communities. I will call this enhancing the *epistemic accountability* of science. In a sense, this combines the epistemic motivation of diversifying the perspectives and values of practicing scientists (the third reason introduced for diversity in science) with the practical and ethical motivation of expanding science's relationship to the public (the fourth reason). The thought here is that ensuring that the perspectives and values of practicing scientists mirror those of diverse social groups and communities can support the production of scientific knowledge that serves those groups and communities. This contributes to science's obligation to generate knowledge and products in society's best interests (see Section 1) – and thus to discharging science's obligation to the public.

Why think greater diversity of practicing scientists can help ensure that scientific advances reflect public priorities, and the priorities of a greater range of communities? This idea relates to considerations of the roles values play in science, particularly how values influence the specifics of research agendas. Recall from Section 3 how scientific understanding is highly specific to its aims. The basic idea of that discussion is that scientists' individual characteristics, including their social identities, can influence their research programs. That influence shapes, first of all, what is investigated – whether to prioritize cancer research or heart disease research, for example – but then also what specifically about those phenomena scientists seek to understand, predict, influence, and so on. Beyond this, the philosophical literature on values in science has mapped many other ways in which the social values of scientists influence research: in how variables are operationalized, evidential standards, and much more (see Elliott, 2022, for an overview). All of this means that stakeholders in science decide (actively or passively) what kinds of scientific knowledge we amass. This is a step beyond the earlier point that a diverse group of scientists is better able to generate legitimate knowledge: the idea here is that the knowledge generated is more reflective of societal concern. This influence of broadened participation in science is explored by Elliott (2017, 2022) and Schroeder (2022), among others.

Consider, as an example, biomedical research on cancer. A significant amount of research has focused on cancer genomics; just one example is the 1.5 billion USD, ten-year Human Cancer Genome Project. Note that it was a choice to invest those funds in cancer genomics rather than into research on social determinants of cancer. This is so for each dollar; it is also so for each newly minted scientist. The scientific establishment can and does pursue both projects. But the investment is more or less zero sum, and social determinants of health tend to get much less investment than genomics. These are two features of cancer that, on purely epistemic grounds, are both worthy of investigation. If the focus is on decreasing cancer burden, social determinants of cancer are clearly the winning research program. A focus on generating advanced cancer treatments or theoretical knowledge of cancer biology instead pushes toward genomics research.

Schroeder (2022) describes how value judgments that influence scientific research can be assessed from a political perspective, including according to whether and to what extent the values are shared by the public. Misalignment between the specific focuses of dominant research agendas and the concerns of public institutions and communities is arguably a failure of science to serve those institutions and communities, and thus to live up to science's obligation to society that I have emphasized. Diverse participation in science can mitigate this by shaping research agendas in ways that reflect the concerns of the diverse communities and public institutions in which scientists participate.

An emphasis on this last reason for diversity in science, what I have called the *epistemic accountability of science*, also has implications for what features of diverse participation in science are important. Insofar as this aim for diversity is endorsed, it is not, sufficient to enable a broader range of professional participants in science; scientists and students with social identities underrepresented in science also must be supported in bringing those identities into their scientific work, to inspire and shape their research priorities. This also may reveal a broader range of social identities that are relevant to representation in professional science, to the extent that various communities and groups that differ along a number of dimensions have distinctive values and interests.

5.2 Participatory Research

Now, let us consider a second form of participation in science: amateur or nonprofessional participation in scientific research. I will use as an umbrella term "participatory research." One might define this as scientific research with any role for members of the public that goes beyond the traditional role as research subjects. The Cornell Lab of Ornithology has a long-running and well-known initiative in which members of the public help to collect data on bird breeding habits, courtship behaviors, habitats, color morphs, and more. Public participation in data-gathering enables the collection of more data and in a broader range of circumstances. In 2012, some communities across Pennsylvania and New York began water-quality monitoring in response to nearby fracking, partnering with scientists with practical impacts for water-quality protection in the region (Kimura and Kinchy, 2019).

The inclusion of public participants in scientific research is well established in some fields, such as ecological research and environmental health, the disciplines of the two examples just mentioned. Participatory research is also gaining traction in a much broader range of fields. The practice can have a range of benefits for research, but its primary appeal is often societal in nature, namely, as a way to increase public accessibility or community impact of the research. As participatory research traditions have developed, different names have been established in different fields and subfields for these practices: citizen science, community science, community-based participatory research, action research, and many more (Vaughn and Jacquez, 2020). These differences in terminology mirror differences in how members of the public tend to be included and with what goals, with one tradition emphasizing augmentation of science's research power and a separate tradition emphasizing the potential for societal impact (Ottinger, 2017).

Thoughtfully pursued participatory research may be uniquely valuable to furthering science's obligation to public needs and interests. The development of participatory research methods in science expands one of the main relationships between science and the public, namely, participation in science (see Figure 1). This expanded participation can, in turn, contribute to improving other relationships between science and the public.

For one thing, participatory research is a marvelous opportunity for increasing public understanding of science. Participatory research projects carried out across a range of scientific disciplines, with a wide variety of focuses and relevant communities, enable members of the public who may never be employed in STEM careers to nonetheless have personal, situated involvement with science in practice. These experiences may contribute to public participants' understanding of scientific methods and their rationale; when science is relevant to their goals; how to seek scientific expertise that furthers those goals; and why, when, and about what to trust scientists – all potential targets for scientific literacy (see Table 2). Deploying participatory research opportunities thoughtfully and systematically in formal science education settings, as they sometimes are, maximizes this potential contribution to public understanding of science.

Participatory research can also expand science's relationship to public communities in a way that goes beyond what is achieved through diversified professional participation, especially regarding how scientific aims reflect community priorities. What I have in mind extends the idea developed in Section 5.1 of importing community values and concerns into science to help science more fully and equitably serve public communities and institutions. Participatory research has the potential to better align scientific research goals with the values and concerns of relevant communities, to the end of making the research more valuable to those communities.

Regardless of background, scientists can be expected to share at least some aims, such as establishing a publication record, advancing knowledge, and perhaps specific aims related to employers or funding bodies (Dunlap et al., 2021). Scientists are also trained into specific cultures of science and medicine, which include professional value systems, expectations regarding communication format and specific professional norms, and what are recognized as legitimate and important questions or goals. These shared aims and cultures are important to scientific success, but they can also limit the influence of divergent community aims and cultures on scientific activity.

In this brief discussion of the potential of participatory research to improve relationships between science and the public, I have assumed that participatory research is carried out in a way that enables the research to reflect community values and the participating public to truly share in the research. These are strong assumptions that go unmet in many participatory research projects. So, I will close this section with a discussion of what is needed for participatory research to play these societal roles, potentially an important contribution to discharging science's obligation to the public.

Consider the question of what value participation in research has for public participants. This value is shaped by the extent of their participation. In some projects, like the Cornell Lab of Ornithology, public participation consists solely in data collection. This is especially common in citizen science projects as practiced in natural science fields like biology and astronomy. At the opposite end of the spectrum, the participating public might be involved from the earliest stages of research design through the full research project, helping to shape research questions, study methods, conclusions drawn, and all the other decisions made along the way. This degree of public participation is perhaps most common in community-based participatory research and action research projects as sometimes practiced in the social sciences and community health research. Another variety of extensive public involvement is when community groups initiate the research, finding scientists willing to work with them on the goals they have already identified. This pattern is exemplified by the water-quality monitoring research mentioned earlier and other research profiled in Kimura and Kinchy (2019). (See Shirk et al., 2012, for a deeper discussion of these types of participatory research.)

What extent of public participation is valuable to the participating public depends on their goals for the research and their participation in it (Kimura and Kinchy, 2016; Dunlap et al., 2021). If, for instance, the participating public is motivated out of sheer interest in the investigation, a desire to be involved in research, or the simple educational goal of exposure to ongoing scientific research activities, involvement solely in data collection can suffice. It is certainly easier to involve public participants, and a greater number of public participants, in this capacity than in more integral roles in research. If, in contrast, participant goals include influencing the specific aims of the research, understanding the research findings, or supporting research directed to social ends they care about, then deeper involvement is necessary.

In some cases, members of the public are motivated to get involved in participatory research not because of any direct benefits to them as participants, but in the hope that their participation increases the value of the research for their community or broader society. When such a motivation is the goal – or one among many goals – then public participants generally must be involved as full research collaborators rather than as mere data collectors. Without equal standing with the professional scientists involved and equal access to information, public participants cannot hope to shape the research in ways that benefit their communities.

The point here, then, is not that maximal public involvement in research is always better but rather that public participation in scientific research is best able to further societal needs by structuring the extent of public participation according to public participants' goals for their participation (Dunlap et al., 2021). Indeed, there are also practical benefits of prioritizing the participating public's goals in research design, as this will make research participation more desirable to potential participants, resulting in the researchers having an easier time of recruiting participation among the public. In summary, scientists developing participatory research projects should consider what the participating public stands to gain directly from their participation in the scientific research, and whether and to what extent their involvement satisfies their goals.

Furthermore, it is best if the goals of potential public participants are not assumed at the outset but rather explicitly analyzed at an early stage of research design (Evans and Potochnik, 2023). This will enable researchers to structure opportunities for public participation such that they are best positioned to meet participants' goals. It also enables the research to reflect the priorities of the public institutions and communities from whom participants are to be drawn. This is essential if participants' goals include impact on their community, and it is essential if participatory research is to be a pathway for the priorities of public institutions and communities to influence scientific research agendas, as suggested earlier in this discussion.

5.3 Participation and Public Trust in Science

So far in this section, I have discussed reasons to expand professional and public participation in scientific research. My main focus has been on how diversifying professional participation in science and participatory scientific research can each enable the scientific enterprise to improve or deepen its relationship to public institutions and communities. Among other relationships between science and the public explored in those sections, I have motivated the idea that both forms of participation can contribute to how well scientific research agendas reflect the goals and concerns of a diverse public. I have also investigated how this idea can bring to light important features of diversity in STEM efforts and of participatory research design. I conclude this section on participation in science by considering the potential of both forms of expanded participation to improve public trust in science.

There are a few ways in which broadened participation in science may support public trust in science. First, I want to return to my focus on how both diversifying science and participatory research support improved alignment of scientific research priorities with societal aims. Diversifying science helps to ensure professional participants in science reflect the full range of social identities across public communities and bring those identities to their research, which will contribute to research aims better reflecting the breadth of priorities in the population at large. Thoughtfully designed participatory research, meanwhile, more directly imports community concerns into research aims and design (Fiorino, 1990). For participatory research, the relevant communities can be directly targeted for inclusion.

Schroeder (2022) helpfully distinguishes between ethical and political approaches to managing values in science: the former involves ethical deliberation to determine the right values, whereas the latter relies on deliberative process to ensure societal responsiveness, setting aside the question of which values are correct. As I have developed the idea here, both diversifying science and participatory methods stand to contribute to the political legitimacy of values in science: both offer means for more effectively incorporating the full range of community values into scientific research. Elliott (2017, 2022) also motivates both of these forms of inclusion in science as ways to ensure scientific research is more responsive to community concerns. He motivates a political rather than an ethical approach insofar as it is difficult to arrive at broadly shared ethical conclusions: "When ethical principles are less settled, science should be influenced as much as possible by values that represent broad societal priorities" (Elliott, 2017, 14).

A second benefit of broadened participation in science for public trust regards transparency. Thoughtfully conducted public participation in research can offer participants insight into all the influences on the research and an opportunity to object to features they deem problematic. Participatory research and diversity in science also offer an indirect form of this benefit to communities in which professional scientists and public participants are embedded. Elliott (2017,

2022) and Schroeder (2022) both emphasize this value of broadened participation in science. As Elliott (2022) puts the point, "When scientists are open about their data, methods, and assumptions, it ideally allows others to recognize how values have influenced scientific work, so they can decide how they want to respond to it (e.g., accepting it, rejecting it, or reinterpreting it)" (46).

For this reason, the open science movement also has been suggested as a way to support increased public participation in science (e.g. Leonelli et al., 2015). Open science is a set of practices to support widespread free access to research findings, including but not limited to open-access publication, where scientific articles are freely viewable online by anyone. Rendering the process and products of scientific research more visible to a broad audience can enable familiarity with research practices that can support research involvement or even research activity conducted wholly outside institutional science. In the context of the present focus on participation in science as facilitating public trust in science, it is worth noting that open science also can increase transparency in science, one of the focuses in Section 4's survey of calls for science to become more trustworthy.

I want to propose that a third benefit broadened participation in science may have for trust in science consists simply in increasing the extent of contact between scientific research and the public (separate from any implications this may have for the management of values or alignment of research with community priorities). As mentioned in Section 5.1, broadened professional participation in STEM increases the contact points with a variety of communities, including those traditionally underrepresented in and underserved by science. Increasing contact between science and the public via participatory research has the potential not only to increase contact points with science but also to disrupt traditional power dynamics that can damage public trust. Direct involvement of public participants in carrying out research and, especially, in designing research conveys that the research belongs to the public. This additional proposed benefit of expanded participation in science consists simply in the sense of inclusion – and the fact of inclusion – in which it results.

Goldenberg (2021) motivates both these forms of broadened participation in science – focusing on health research and practice in particular – as necessary means toward addressing the crisis in public trust she diagnoses (see Section 4). She suggests that the benefits of diversity include greater sociocultural competencies to work with a diverse public, as well as "challenging entrenched attitudes and practices" in professional health research and care settings that are problematic (181). Goldenberg emphasizes the potential for community participation in research and practice to "further health equity goals not only by crafting and honing effective interventions but also by empowering members of underrepresented communities" (181).

In sum, the benefits that further diversifying professional participation in science and expanding effective use of participatory research methods may have for public trust in science include making science more inclusive, more transparent, and its findings more just. (The order of these is reversed from how I introduced them.) Greater inclusivity results from expanding the range of people with direct or indirect grounds for believing scientific research is shaped by their communities. Greater transparency results from opening windows onto processes of scientific research and providing opportunities to shape its trajectory. And greater justice of scientific findings is procedural, resulting from maximizing routes whereby the concerns of relevant communities, even if those concerns vary and shift over time, can effectively influence scientific research. Each of these benefits makes science more worthy of public trust, and, beyond improving science's trustworthiness, inclusivity, and transparency, also creates opportunities for greater trust to be cultivated.

Both forms of participation – diversifying professional participation in science and including community members as partners in research – are current priorities and practices in at least some parts of the scientific enterprise. These are thus real means at science's disposal in the project of improving its relationship to public institutions and communities. Taken together and working in tandem, these have the promise to be a vehicle for improving science's trustworthiness and public trust in science. Other institutional changes to science might still be needed to bolster public trust, but broadened participation in science stands to address at least some of the needs for increasing trust in science identified in Section 4.

6 Science in Service to the Public

In Section 1, I argued that the scientific enterprise bears an obligation to public institutions and communities in virtue of its societal support, its societal value, and its contributions to societal problems. Section 2 detailed the interrelationships among science, philosophy, and the public in early twentieth-century Vienna, as a model of deep interrelationships among disciplines and public discourse and concern, to expand our sense of possibility for these relationships. The current limited modes of public engagement with science (and philosophy thereof) are not necessary and, in fact, have been very different – at a time when science, philosophy, and society were all undergoing dramatic change. Subsequent Sections, 3, 4, and 5, examined, in turn, public understanding of science, public trust in science, and public participation in science. These sections provide resources for a deeper consideration of science's obligation to the public, as introduced in Section 1. This final section thus ends by returning to the question of science's obligation to the public.

In Section 6.1, I suggest Section 5's conclusions regarding the value of broadened participation in science as a way for public communities to play a greater role in shaping scientific research priorities. This inspires an approach to determining scientific research priorities that I call *responsive science*. In Section 6.2, I more fully develop an account of how responsive science shapes scientific priorities by addressing two concerns about this approach. Finally, Section 6.3 examines how responsive science and other resources introduced in this Element help clarify and address science's obligation to the public. I conclude by considering more fully the roles philosophers of science in particular can play in fulfilling this obligation.

6.1 Responsive Science

An inescapable question about science concerns what research aims should be pursued. This question occurs in at least two forms: first, it seems some research aims should be off the table entirely, objectionable on empirical or ethical grounds; second, there is always a question of where to invest resources. These resources include monetary investment, like grant funding and research infrastructure, as well as human capital – what scientists are trained and encouraged to study. The idea raised in Section 3 that subtle differences in specific research aims in turn influence the nature of the findings (as developed in Potochnik, 2017) only amplifies the significance of these questions about which research aims should be pursued, and to what extent. In my view, these questions about research priorities deserve much more explicit consideration in the institutions of science as well as in public discourse than they typically receive.

Philip Kitcher, among others, appreciates the need for scientific research questions to be responsive to public interest. Kitcher (2001) suggests a hypothetical process of "ideal deliberation" that involves training up a representative group in the details of scientific inquiry, then seeking their consensus on priorities for scientific research. Their deliberation is to take into consideration not only the interests of their group but also the interests of others they represent and future generations as well. Science is *well ordered*, Kitcher claims, when its research priorities match what such an ideal deliberation would entail.

In Section 5, I explored how continued efforts to diversify professional participation in science and to engage public participation in research might lead scientific research priorities to better reflect the priorities of diverse public communities. If this is right, then broadened participation in science is poised to contribute toward answering these questions about research priorities, as then science will to some extent take on research priorities that reflect the priorities of public institutions and communities, in all their variety. This proposal has something in common with Kitcher's project. My proposal is a suggestion for how scientific research can achieve a better match between scientific research priorities and public interest. And, like Kitcher's project, I suggest that achieving such a match would improve science's ethical standing, making it more worthy of public trust and investment. In light of these similarities, I want to point out what I think are some advantages of the proposal I have sketched in comparison to Kitcher's vision of well-ordered science.

Kitcher's proposal for determining what scientific research should be prioritized imports resources from political philosophy into philosophy of science, insofar as it employs ideal theory. Ideal theory is an approach of considering idealized agents and social and reasoning processes so as to identify an ideal end point that can serve as a normative goal, a regulative ideal. Ideal theory is in some ways similar to how idealized representation is used in science to determine behaviors that more complex, real systems only approximate – as with the ideal gas law. The difference is that, with ideal theory in political philosophy, the end point is not just thought to be an approximation but is taken on as an ideal to be pursued (Mills, 2005).

In my view, ideal theory, whatever its merits, is the wrong tool for the job when considering what scientific research should be pursued. The value of ideal theory consists in its ability to accommodate divergent values and circumstances that must be transcended if a single ideal end point is to be found. (See Mills, 2005, for concerns about ideal theory as a tool even in this context of moral theorizing.) Thankfully, identifying such an ideal end point, a static description of well-ordered science, is not necessary for science. For one thing, the epistemic and social landscape in which scientific research occurs is always shifting. Scientific advances and breakthroughs change the epistemic landscape for future research projects, while political changes and shifting societal needs change the social landscape for such projects. Thus, how scientific research should be focused should be expected to be in a state of continuous change and constant renegotiation rather than approaching an ideal that incorporates the viewpoints of all present and future stakeholders. The concern here is not that ideal theory cannot accommodate changing conditions but rather that continual change makes it unnecessary to identify a single, just distribution of research priorities.

Further, even at a given point in time, there is no need to identify a single ideal distribution of scientific research priorities. In political theory, this is sometimes taken to be necessary insofar as a community of individuals needs to agree to a single form of governance. No such centralized coordination or agreement is needed among those pursuing scientific research. Instead, each individual participant in science can make decisions that influence the overall distribution of research priorities – about their next research priorities, what degree program to pursue, what grants to fund, and more – without awareness of the best overall distribution of research priorities, so long as a mechanism exists for the resulting distribution to be just. What is needed is not centralized coordination but localized adjustment. Indeed, centralized coordination or a centralized vision is made especially difficult by the wide range of scientific research and the wide range of community concerns this research may relate to.

Because of the diversity of social communities and scientific research projects and the continuously evolving nature of both science and society, an ideal end point is not a helpful concept for theorizing the normative considerations at play for scientific research pursuits. What is needed is not a hypothetical agreement to specify an ideal end point but, instead, procedures: ways to adjust the institution of science so that it better connects to and reflects the values and priorities of public institutions and communities, in all their variety. Diverse professional participation in science and expanded public participation in science, I suggest, can play this role. In contrast to Kitcher's goal of well-ordered science, I term this proposal *responsive science.*

Responsive science is a proposal for what Schroeder (2022) calls a political approach to managing values in science (or, at least, one basic role of values – determining the research agenda). Ethical approaches to managing values attempt to determine the right values to be pursued, whereas political approaches attempt to follow legitimate procedures for managing values. What I have dubbed responsive science is a proposal for ensuring scientific research priorities are responsive to societal and community needs via, first, diversifying professional participation in science so that this participation is representative of all relevant communities and, second, incorporating sufficient public participation in scientific research so that community priorities effectively shape research goals. Note also that I take the relevance of social identities to be broader than simply values. Hilligardt (2022) argues that science is influenced by more than social values; she suggests the influence also includes social perspectives, opinions, and interests. Thus, though I refer to "values" when addressing arguments specifically targeting values in science, elsewhere I refer broadly to "values and perspectives," and similar.

Elliott (2022) evaluates ethical versus political approaches to managing values in science. One concern he raises is that value judgments pervade scientific research to such an extent that identifying one political procedure to govern these judgments would be very difficult. (I address other concerns Elliott raises in Section 6.2.) In my proposal of responsive science, sufficiently broad participation in science itself constitutes the procedure. There is no need to specify an additional political procedure to adjudicate the roles of values, at least in determining research priorities, beyond the in-practice give-and-take among (an adequately diverse body of) professional scientists as well as their (sufficiently included and empowered) public collaborators. Recall from Section 4 that adequate diversity requires support for bringing one's full identity to one's scientific research, and sufficiently included and empowered public collaborators requires depth of inclusion appropriate to the public participants' aims for their participation and for the research itself. So, the requirement of sufficiently broad participation in science is a strong requirement. An advantage of relying on broad professional and public participation in science to align scientific priorities with public priorities is that the process occurs automatically when conducting science structured in this way.

I do not claim that what I have termed responsive science has the power to resolve all needs to regulate the roles of values in science nor that it fully addresses how scientific research should respond to societal need. At the very least, the social structure of science must adequately support the necessary give-and-take among scientists and participating members of the public (Longino, 1990, 2002). For some research topics, other forms of public input may also be important (Fiorino, 1990). I also think society would benefit from a more robust, ongoing public conversation about what scientific research goals to prioritize. But I do propose that responsive science – diversified professional participation in science coupled with sufficient public participation in scientific research – is an important tool for aligning scientific priorities with public priorities. Responsive science uses a political approach of specifying process rather than goal, and it does not rely on an idealized procedure of achieving agreement. Creating responsive science via broadened inclusion is, I suggest, an important means to shifting institutional science toward science in service to the public.

6.2 Legitimate Scientific Priorities

In Section 6.1, I used resources developed in Section 5 to propose a strategy for just determination of scientific research priorities that I called *responsive science*. Here, I more fully develop an account of how responsive science shapes scientific priorities by addressing two concerns one might have with that strategy. One concern someone might have with my proposal of responsive science is that scientific research priorities being shaped by public priorities in this way might lead science to focus too fully on applied research with clear practical application rather than visionary basic research. I will call this *the problem of dark matter research*, as I can imagine highly theoretical cosmological research is one research priority potentially overlooked by members of the public untrained in science and facing a litany of real-world problems. A second concern someone might have is that, if science better reflects the full range of social values held by one or another community, it may inherit pernicious priorities from some segments of the public. This is the worry that the political approach to managing values offered by responsive science is not sufficient to guarantee that science is shaped only by ethically acceptable values. Let us call this *the problem of pernicious priorities*.

What I have called the problem of dark matter research is the worry that, if scientific research priorities are increasingly yoked to matters of public concern, those priorities will become ever-more practical and applied, and science will miss out on investigating fundamental questions about the universe and life, as well as any basic research where practical applications are not yet obvious. I think, to some extent, we might indeed anticipate such a shift. Surely, aiming for scientific research priorities to reflect public priorities would inspire a relative shift of resources away from research focused purely on abstract understanding toward research with application for social benefit. Consider the billions of dollars spent on cancer genomics research compared to the relatively small amount of funding dedicated to public health research into social determinates of cancer and other diseases, like poverty, healthcare access, and environmental injustice. To the extent that cancer researchers come from underserved communities facing these challenges and public participation is sought from such communities, we can expect a shift of resources and attention toward social barriers to health. If so, that is okay – or, better put: that is just.

In this context, it is also helpful to recall that responsive science obviates a need for uniform agreement on research priorities. To take the example of cancer research, a shift of resources toward social determinates of health does not mean that cancer genomics research comes to an end. There will no doubt continue to be public demand for advanced cancer treatments, many of which rely on genomics research. Further, genetics and genomics research has only grown as a research priority, in several fields of science, over the past several decades. A relative shift of resources toward research with equitable public benefit does not entail the abandonment of other research priorities.

Taken to its logical conclusion, does responsive science as I have described it involve science abandoning the pursuit of pure knowledge, that is, research pursuits without any apparent practical applications? I think there is abundant evidence that this would not be the result. For one thing, love of uncovering mysteries about our universe, from the cosmos to genes, is a value shared among professional participants in science across a wide variety of backgrounds and social identities. Nor is this sense of awe about our world and drive to understand more about it the special purview of scientists; these priorities are shared with a sizeable segment of the public. For example, Zooniverse, the largest internet platform for participatory research, features more than twenty participatory research projects in cosmology and astrophysics (as of May 2023).[7] Again, it may be that aligning scientific priorities more fully with public priorities shifts resources and attention more toward research with tangible benefits, but there is no reason to think that basic research for the sake of human understanding will cease.

As a reminder, responsive science is the proposal that a properly inclusive cadre of professional scientists, engaging relevant public communities in research those communities value, will organically result in a just alignment of research priorities with public concerns. This can be anticipated to result in a relative shift of investment toward research with practical and equitable applications, but there is no reason to think this will reduce the variety of research pursued or eliminate the pursuit of pure, theoretical knowledge. Further, as science contributes to addressing inequities and social needs, the balance of scientific research priorities can be expected to shift accordingly, as community values and concerns change with amelioration of inequalities.

Let us turn now to the second potential concern I said I would address, what I called the problem of pernicious priorities. One might have a concern about scientific research priorities being yoked to the fads and passing interests of communities that are by and large scientifically untrained or, worse, to problematic values present in some communities. If responsive science relies solely on a procedural approach to determining research priorities, merely taking on the priorities of broader public communities, then what can ensure that scientific research – or at least some of it – is not driven by prejudices, ignorance, and unethical values, which are surely present in many communities? Note that science has faced this problem throughout its history. Examples of past sexist and racist research priorities, as well as research based on passing fads and predicated on erroneous belief, are numerous. So, the question is not whether responsive science would introduce a problem of pernicious values but rather whether it would exacerbate or ameliorate it.

Recall from Section 5 that one main advantage touted for increasing diversity in science is the epistemic and ethical improvement provided by more robust critique of scientific research from a wider variety of perspectives (Longino, 1990, 2002; Elliott, 2022; Schroeder, 2022). This is a means by which continuing to diversify professional participation in science can be expected to ameliorate pernicious values influencing research aims. Further, scientists will continue to be trained into the shared professional aims and cultures of science,

---

[7] Zooniverse website: www.zooniverse.org.

which will be a mediating influence on the priorities influencing their work – both their priorities and also the priorities introduced via public participation. Priorities of public participants that do not reflect the present state of scientific knowledge or that are unethical or unjust will face scrutiny by the scientists with which they collaborate. The judgments of such mediating scientists are in turn indirectly shaped by professional norms to which they are subject. Existing training in the responsible conduct of research can be thoughtfully designed to better support this role for professional norms.

This highlights the importance of the two-part structure of my characterization of responsive science, depicted visually in Figure 3. This includes, on the one hand, (a) bidirectional influence between science's professional norms and a sufficiently diverse and inclusive community of professional scientists; and, on the other hand, (b) the influence of communities motivated to engage and participate in various research projects on scientists that share or appreciate aspects of their identities or values. The former, (a), ameliorates pernicious values influencing the research aims of the scientific establishment, while also mediating the research priorities of scientists with a broad range of social identities and of the communities with which they collaborate. The latter, (b), dampens the influence of the scientific establishment by creating inroads for community priorities to shape scientific priorities. The diversity of professional scientists, with different social identities, ensures diverse communities can exert this influence. As noted in Section 6.1, the structure of responsive science would not obviate the need for communities and society at large to interrogate their values and ethical principles. But it would provide a mechanism for scientific research to respond to

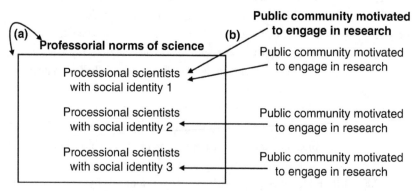

Figure 3 Responsive science involves (a) bidirectional influence between science's professional norms and a diverse community of professional scientists and (b) the influence of communities motivated to engage in some scientific research project on scientists that share or appreciate their identities or values.

the values and priorities of a robust variety of communities, while mediating the influence of those values and priorities on science with both established scientific norms and the values and concerns of other communities.

This characterization of responsive science and how it limits the influence of pernicious priorities still leaves one related concern unaddressed. Can responsive science, as I have described it, ensure that the proper communities influence scientific research? Another concern Elliott (2022) raises about political approaches, such as responsive science, to managing values in science is the difficulty of determining which communities' values should influence some research. A variety of this concern applies in the context of the problem of pernicious priorities, especially regarding how public participants shape scientific research priorities. To return to the example of cancer research, how should scientists determine if the relevant population for their research is people in underserved communities at heightened risk for cancer or people diagnosed with cancer seeking medical treatment? The concerns of these communities pull cancer research in different directions.

Part of the answer to this concern is, as already described, that there does not need to be a single answer. Some scientists, with one constellation of interests and values, will engage with the former communities, while others, with a different set of interests and values, will engage with the latter communities. This variety is assured by achieving a sufficiently diverse group of professional scientists.

Yet, in some cases, we may think certain communities should not influence scientific research at all. While it is acceptable that some scientists will research social determinates of cancer while others will research medical treatments for cancer, the same is not the case for, say, research into the value of gender-affirming mental health support for gender-diverse individuals versus research into more effective approaches to conversion therapy. Conversion therapy is the widely debunked practice of attempting to change a person's sexual orientation or gender identity. Conducting additional scientific research into conversion therapy's effectiveness would be unethical due to its significant recognized harms and would also be predicated on a misunderstanding of relevant scientific findings. So, what if eager public participants in scientific research into mental health and gender diversity urge conversion therapy as a research priority?

Here too, the advocate of responsive science can turn to the professional norms to which scientists are subject for solution. Professional scientists and the disciplinary norms of science structure public participation in science. If the professional scientific community is adequately diverse, this paves the way for the control of imported public priorities so that vulnerable stakeholders are protected and current scientific knowledge is heeded. This challenge further illustrates the value of the two-part structure of responsive science, the intersection of diverse professional participation in science and broad public participation.

As noted in Section 5, sufficient diversity among professional scientists also requires diversifying scientific norms and institutions away from the Western dominance we see at present. This is advanced in part by expanding participatory research approaches, especially those approaches that aim to incorporate public participants' priorities and perspectives, as an alternative to "parachute research" often conducted in the Global South (Sanches de Oliveira and Baggs, 2023). Here too, the value of the two-part structure of responsive science is apparent.

This two-part structure also has implications for how participatory research should be structured. First, this suggests that truly collaborative participatory research is epistemically and ethically preferable to research occurring wholly outside institutionalized science. Even as public concerns should influence research priorities, engagement with professional scientists and the institutional norms of science are important for constraining the nature of that influence. Second, this suggests the need for participatory research opportunities to be thoughtfully developed to achieve engagement with the intended communities and incorporate their concerns. In Section 5, I pointed out that how research participation opportunities are structured influences who will participate. If participatory research activities are to serve as the means for scientific research to respond to public priorities, as I suggest here, scientists must structure opportunities for public participation thoughtfully, as this has ethical implications by shaping which communities' values are reflected in the research.

One might wonder whether my proposal of responsive science entails that all scientific research must include public participation. I do not think this follows. Instead, the role public participation in scientific research plays in responsive science suggests a guideline for when research should be participatory. Public participation should be incorporated in a research project when that participation meaningfully advances the researchers' goals or the goals of some public communities. A sufficiently diverse cadre of professional scientists can help achieve this breadth of participatory research by ensuring a broad range of communities' goals are recognized, or even shared, by at least some scientific researchers.

In this section and Section 6.1, I have built upon Section 5's discussion of broadened participation in science to suggest that such broadened participation can generate *responsive science*, a political approach to a more just distribution of resources and attention across scientific research priorities. I have not demonstrated that responsive science suffices by itself to control the influence of values on science. But I have argued that this strategic use of broadened participation can be expected to ameliorate existing pernicious priorities in science rather than exacerbate them. I suggest that this is a central reason to prioritize broadened participation in science, professional and public, and for the recognition that broadened participation is a tool for better managing the relationship scientific research priorities bear to public concern. Responsive science is a means for science to become more accountable to the public and, accordingly, more worthy of the public's trust.

6.3 Fulfilling Science's Obligation to the Public

In this final section, I want to return to the statement of science's obligation to the public from Section 1 to assess what resources the discussions in this Element have provided for discharging that obligation. In the earlier discussion, I had suggested three features of science as the sources of an institutional obligation to the public: its societal investment (a social benefit), its practical and epistemic value (a capacity to contribute to society), and its contributions to social problems (a social debt). In virtue of what they have received, what they can contribute, and what they owe, the institutions of science have special obligations to society – in particular, obligations to engineer its relationship to public institutions and communities. In Table 1, reproduced here as Table 4, I propose types of obligations in response to specific sources of societal obligation. (Refer back to Section 1.2 for details about these posited obligations, including how obligations vary across disciplines.)

Table 4 Relationships among the sources of science's societal obligations, and the nature of those obligations.

Source of obligation	Variety of source	Type of obligation
Societal investment	Monetary investment in research	Advances of societal worth
	Educational investment	Career pathways; public access to science's value, such as knowledge and skills
Societal value	Epistemic value	Knowledge and products that advance society's best interests;
	Practical value	cultivating trustworthiness
Contributions to social problems	Social inequality	Ameliorating inequalities
	Problematic innovations	Ameliorating detrimental effects

The discussions in previous sections provide additional resources for understanding these various types of obligation and how they may be discharged. To begin with, Section 2's discussion of the Vienna Circle provides a model showing how there can be much deeper interrelationships between science and society, and the philosophy of science, than at present. This highlights how satisfying obligations to the public, including, especially, providing public access to science's value, may be more continuous with scientific research than at present.

On my account, it is educational investment in science that creates the obligation to provide public access to science's value. One interpretation of that obligation, or an aspect of it, is that the institution of science should provide the public with scientific understanding valuable to addressing public needs – both individual and aggregate. Formal and informal opportunities for science education are not incidental to the scientific enterprise, but crucial for discharging its obligation to society. Further, the value of science education consists not only in creating pathways for professional participation in science, but also in supporting public understanding of and public trust in science. One lesson from Section 3 is that effective support for public understanding of science requires careful attention to the specific goal(s) of understanding, that is, to what it is about science that it is valuable for the public to understand. It also must not be neglected that understanding is just one feature of a constellation of attitudes toward science any individual has; others include level of trust, interest, personal connection, and more. Science education has the power, and the obligation, to target all of these attitudes.

I also suggest in Section 1's discussion of obligations that science has the obligation to cultivate its trustworthiness in virtue of its epistemic and practical value to society. Discussions in Section 4 reveal that this is not a simple matter of counteracting science denial, but a deeper project of shoring up the trustworthiness of science and effective public communication of this trustworthiness. That is a challenging and ongoing project; some suggestions for what to attend to appear in Section 4.3. In Section 5, I explore the extent to which diversifying professional participation in science and expanding public participation in science can contribute to this project of increasing science's trustworthiness. Another aspect of cultivating trust in science is effective science communication. Scientists and others engaged professionally with science in the academy and in public-facing positions must work to provide credible and relevant scientific expertise and equitable, depoliticized ways to access this expertise. In today's climate of politicized science, that must involve attending to the framing of messages, so that scientific expertise is not seen to be aligned with just one political outlook or with only some communities.

I have mentioned already in this examination of resources for discharging science's obligations the potential for broadened participation in science to support public trust in science. Beyond that, diversifying professional participation in science and expanding and diversifying public participation can contribute to discharging science's obligations to ameliorate inequalities and the detrimental effects of science: through sheer inclusion in the goods of science, as well as in better reflecting its social priorities. Diversifying professional participation in science also contributes to equitably providing career pathways, and both contribute to fulfilling the obligation of broadening public access to science's value through inclusion and via science's increased responsiveness to community priorities. So much of this relates back to ensuring the values and needs of the public – in all their varieties – influence scientific research and its relationship to the public. This is what I have termed *responsive science*. If my conjecture about the value of responsive science is correct, then this also contributes to discharging science's obligation to provide knowledge and products that advance society's best interests.

This summarizes the theoretical resources surveyed in this Element for discharging the obligations I posited of science toward the public. What is needed to effectively discharge these many aspects of science's obligation to the public is an endeavor involving (at least) the collaborative participation of multiple disciplines, including natural scientists, data from social sciences, and partnership with communities and relevant practitioners outside the academy. This is because skills and bodies of knowledge from a range of disciplines bear on effectively evaluating and responding to science's obligation to society, what in Section 1 I termed *public engagement with science*. A new interdisciplinary series, Cambridge Elements in Public Engagement with Science, which I edit together with Melissa Jacquart, aims to support interdisciplinary exchanges to promote this project.

Although the focus of this Element has been broadly on the relationship between science and the public, the approach and literature emphasis have been philosophical. I will close with a note on roles in the challenging project of public engagement with science for philosophers of science in particular. Philosophy of science can help respond to this obligation of science to the public by theorizing the relationship between science and the public, as in this Element and much research by other authors, some of which has been discussed here. Brigandt (2022), for example, introduces a special issue of the *Canadian Journal of Philosophy* laying the groundwork and exemplifying such philosophical contributions, including some work in partnership with scientists.

But our field can and should do more. Recall from Section 2 the tight interconnections philosophy of science in early twentieth-century Vienna had with a variety of fields of science, its contributions to public discourse, and its attention to political and social concerns. I do not suggest that today's philosophy of science should, or even could, replicate that model. But philosophers of science can direct more attention and collaborative efforts outward, beyond our field, than has been the norm for most of the past century. We are seeing shifts in this direction (Plaisance and Elliott, 2022). Philosophers of science are increasingly embedded in the sciences, contributing to scientific progress (Laplane et al., 2019) and helping to guide interdisciplinary collaboration (e.g. Hubbs et al., 2020). Philosophers of science are also increasingly involved in the research, teaching, and practice of public engagement with science, such as Kristen Intemann's Center for Science, Technology, Ethics and Society at Montana State University; Evelyn Brister's work with the Public Philosophy Network; and my work, along with collaborators, at the University of Cincinnati's Center for Public Engagement with Science, to name just a few.[8] The example of the Vienna Circle reveals that, as philosophy gets more deeply engaged with scientific research, both are better positioned to effectively engage with the public.

The many facets of the relationship between science and the public are increasingly focal in philosophy of science. In this Element, I have explored a range of topics about science and the public that philosophers of science are exploring in their research – and that warrant additional philosophical exploration. I have also suggested that these topics should not simply inspire additional philosophical research but also contribute to philosophy of science looking outward to new audiences and collaborators, to assist in discharging science's obligations to the public.

---

[8] Montana State University Center for Science, Technology, Ethics and Society: https://wetlands.msuextension.org/stes/; Public Philosophy Network: www.publicphilosophynetwork.net; University of Cincinnati Center for Public Engagement with Science: https://ucengagingscience.org.

References

Anderson, Elizabeth, 2011. "Democracy, Public Policy, and Lay Assessments of Scientific Testimony." *Episteme* 8:144–164.

Bardon, Adrian, 2020. *The Truth about Denial: Bias and Self-Deception in Science, Politics, and Religion*. Oxford University Press.

Besley, John C. and Derek Hill, 2020. "Science and Technology: Public Attitudes, Knowledge, and Interest." NSF Science and Engineering Indicators. https://ncses.nsf.gov/pubs/nsb20207/public-familiarity-with-s-t-facts.

Brigandt, Ingo. 2022. "Engaging with Science, Values, and Society: Introduction." *Canadian Journal of Philosophy* 52: 223–226.

Bright, Liam K. 2018. "Du Bois' Democratic Defence of the Value Free Ideal." *Synthese* 195: 2227–2245.

Carnap, Rudolf. 1928. *Der Logische Aufbau der Welt. Translated by Rolf A. George, republished in The Logical Structure of the World and Pseudoproblems in Philosophy*. Open Court (2003).

Cartieri, Francis and Angela Potochnik. 2013. "Toward Philosophy of Science's Social Engagement." *Erkenntnis* 79: 901–916.

Carnap, Rudolf. 1932. "The Elimination of Metaphysics through Logical Analysis of Language." *Erkenntnis* II: 60–81. Translated into English by Arthur Pap in A. J. Ayer (ed.), *Language, Truth, and Logic*. Dover (1936).

Cartwright, Nancy, Jordi Cat, Lola Fleck, and Thomas E. Uebel. 1996. *Otto Neurath: Philosophy between Science and Politics*. Cambridge University Press.

Chakravartty, Anjan. 2022. "Scientific Knowledge vs. Knowledge of Science." *Science & Education*. https://doi.org/10.1007/s11191-022-00376-6.

Conix, Stijn, Olivier Lemeire, and Pei-Shan Chi. 2022. "The Public Relevance of Philosophy." *Synthese* 200(1): 1–28.

"Constitution and By-Laws of the Philosophy of Science Association." 1948. *Philosophy of Science* 15: 176–177.

de Melo-Martín, Inmaculada and Kristen Intemann. 2018. *The Fight against Doubt: How to Bridge the Gap between Scientists and the Public*. Oxford University Press.

De Regt, Henk W. 2017. *Understanding Scientific Understanding*. Oxford University Press.

Douglas, Heather E. 2009. *Science, Policy, and the Value-Free Ideal*. University of Pittsburgh Press.

Douglas, Heather E. 2013. "The Moral Terrain of Science." *Erkenntnis* 79: 961–979.

Douglas, Heather E. 2022. "Institutions and the Division of Ethical Labor in Science." Philosophy of Science Association Biennial Meeting, Pittsburgh, PA, November 12.

Dunlap, Lucas, Amanda Corris, Melissa Jacquart, Zvi Biener, and Angela Potochnik. 2021. "Divergence of Values and Goals in Participatory Research." *Studies in History and Philosophy of Science Part A* 88: 284–291.

Edmonds, David. 2020. *The Murder of Professor Schlick: The Rise and Fall of the Vienna Circle*. Princeton University Press.

Elgin, Catherine Z. 2017. *True Enough*. MIT Press.

Elliott, Kevin. 2017. *A Tapestry of Values*. Oxford University Press.

Elliott, Kevin. 2022. *Values in Science*. Elements in Philosophy of Science, Cambridge University Press.

Evans, Andrew and Angela Potochnik. 2023. "Theorizing Participatory Research." In Emily Anderson (ed.),*Ethical Issues in Stakeholder-Engaged Health Research*. Springer.

Fehr, Carla and Kathryn S. Plaisance. 2010. "Socially Relevant Philosophy of Science: An Introduction." *Synthese* 177: 301–316.

Feinstein, Noah. 2011. "Salvaging Science Literacy." *Science Education* 95: 168–185.

Fiorino, Daniel J. 1990. "Citizen Participation and Environmental Risk: A Survey of Institutional Mechanisms." *Science, Technology, & Human Values* 15: 226–243.

Fleisher, Will and Dunja Šešelja. 2023. "Responsibility for Collective Epistemic Harms." *Philosophy of Science* 90: 1–20.

Friedman, Michael. 1996. "Overcoming Metaphysics: Carnap and Heidegger." In Ronald N. Giere, Herbert Feigl and Alan Richardson (eds.), *Origins of Logical Empiricism*. New ed. Vol. 16. University of Minnesota Press, 45–79.

Friedman, Michael. 2000. *A Parting of the Ways: Carnap, Cassirer, and Heidegger*. Open Court.

Friedman, Michael. 2007. "Coordination, Constitution, and Convention: The Evolution of the A Priori in Logical Empiricism." In Thomas E. Uebel and Alan W. Richardson (eds.), *The Cambridge Companion to Logical Empiricism*, 91–116. Cambridge University Press.

Fyfe, Aileen. 2017. "How Did the Royal Society Cope with Increasing Specialization?" *A History of Scientific Journals*, December 30, accessed August 23, 2022. https://arts.st-andrews.ac.uk/philosophicaltransactions/how-did-the-society-deal-with-increasing-specialization/.

Gaieck, William, J. P. Lawrence, Maria Montchal, William Pandori, and Evelyn Valdez-Ward. 2020. "Opinion: Science Policy for Scientists: A Simple Task for Great Effect." *Proceedings of the National Academy of Sciences of the United States of America* 117: 20977–20981.

Galison, Peter. 1990. "Aufbau/Bauhaus: Logical Positivism and Architectural Modernism." *Critical Inquiry* 16(4): 709–752.

Goldenberg, Maya J. 2021. *Vaccine Hesitancy: Public Trust, Expertise, and the War on Science*. University of Pittsburgh Press.

Goldenberg, Maya J. 2023. "Public Trust in Science." *Interdisciplinary Science Reviews* 48(2): 366–378. https://doi.org/10.1080/03080188.2022.2152243.

Grimm, Stephen R. 2012. "The Value of Understanding." *Philosophy Compass* 7: 103–117.

Grimm, Stephen. 2021. "Understanding." In Edward N. Zalta (ed.), *Stanford Encyclopedia of Philosophy* (Summer edition). https://plato.stanford.edu/archives/sum2021/entries/understanding/.

Gustafson, Abel, Matthew H. Goldberg, John E. Kotcher, et al. 2020. "Republicans and Democrats Differ in Why They Support Renewable Energy." *Energy Policy* 141: 111448.

Hahn, Hans, Otto Neurath, and Rudolf Carnap. 1929. "Wissenschaftliche Weltauffassung der Wiener Kreis." Translated in Sahotra Sarkar (ed.), *The Emergence of Logical Empiricism: From 1900 to the Vienna Circle* (Vol. 1). Taylor & Francis (1996), 299–318.

Halpern, Megan K. and Kevin C. Elliott. 2022. "Science as Experience: A Deweyan Model of Science Communication." *Perspectives on Science* 30: 621–656.

Harding, Sandra. 1991. *Whose Science? Whose Knowledge? Thinking from Women's Lives*. Cornell University Press.

Hempel, Carl Gustav. 1965. *Aspects of Scientific Explanation and Other Essays in the Philosophy of Science*. Free Press.

Hilligardt, Hannah. 2022. "Looking beyond Values: The Legitimacy of Social Perspectives, Opinions and Interests in Science." *European Journal for Philosophy of Science* 12: 58.

Hofer, Veronika. 2002. "Philosophy of Biology around the Vienna Circle: Ludwig von Bertalanffy, Joseph Henry Woodger and Philipp Frank. " In Michael Heidelberger and Friedrich Stadler (eds.), *History of Philosophy of Science*. Vienna Circle Institute Yearbook, Vol. 9. Springer, 325–333.

Howard, Don. 2003. "Two Left Turns Make a Right: On the Curious Political Career of North American Philosophy of Science at Mid-century." In Alan Richardson and Gary Hardcastle (eds.), *Logical Empiricism in North America*, 25–93. University of Minnesota Press.

Hubbs, Graham, Michael O'Rourke, and Steven Hecht Orzack. 2020. *The Toolbox Dialogue Initiative: The Power of Cross-Disciplinary Practice.* Routledge.

Kahan, Dan M. 2017. "'Ordinary Science Intelligence': A Science-Comprehension Measure for Study of Risk and Science Communication, with Notes on Evolution and Climate Change." *Journal of Risk Research* 20(8): 995–1016.

Keren, Arnon (2018). "The Public Understanding of What? Laypersons' Epistemic Needs, the Division of Cognitive Labor, and the Demarcation of Science." *Philosophy of Science* 85(5): 781–792.

Khalifa, Kareem (2017). *Understanding, Explanation, and Scientific Knowledge.* Cambridge: Cambridge University Press.

Kimura, Aya H. and Abby Kinchy. 2016. "Citizen Science: Probing the Virtues and Contexts of Participatory Research." *Engaging Science, Technology, and Society* 2: 331–361.

Kimura, Aya H. and Abby Kinchy. 2019. *Science by the People: Participation, Power, and the Politics of Environmental Knowledge.* Rutgers University Press.

Kitcher, Philip. 2001. *Science, Truth, and Democracy.* Oxford Studies in Philosophy of Science. Oxford University Press.

Laplane, Lucie, Paolo Mantovani, Ralph Adolphs, et al. 2019. "Why Science Needs Philosophy." *Proceedings of the National Academy of Science* 116: 3948–3952.

Leonelli, Sabina, Daniel Spichtinger, and Barbara Prainsack. 2015. "Sticks and Carrots: Encouraging Open Science at Its Source." *Geography and Environment* 2: 12–16.

Longino, Helen. 1990. *Science as Social Knowledge.* Indiana University Press.

Longino, Helen. 2002. *The Fate of Knowledge.* Princeton University Press.

McCright, Aaron, Katherine Dentzman, Meghan Charters, and Thomas Dietz. 2013. "The Influence of Political Ideology on Trust in Science." *Environmental Research Letters* 8: 1–9.

McIntyre, Lee. 2021. *How to Talk to a Science Denier: Conversations with Flat Earthers, Climate Deniers, and Others Who Defy Reason.* MIT Press.

Miller, Steve. 2001. "Public Understanding of Science at the Crossroads." *Public Understanding of Science* 10(1): 115–120.

Mills, Charles W. 2005. "'Ideal Theory' as Ideology." *Hypatia* 20: 165–184.

Neurath, Marie and Robin Kinross. 2009. *The Transformer: Principles of Making Isotype Charts.* Hyphen Press.

Neurath, Otto. 1932. "Protokollsätze." *Erkenntnis* 3 (1): 204–214.

Neurath, Otto. 1939. *Modern Man in the Making.* Knopf.

O'Connor, Cailin and James Owen Weatherall. 2019. *The Misinformation Age: How False Beliefs Spread.* Yale University Press.

OECD. 2019. "PISA 2018 Science Framework." In PISA 2018 Assessment and Analytical Framework. OECD Publishing. *https://doi.org/10.1787/f30da688-en.*

Office of Science and Technology Policy. 2021. *Progress Report on the Implementaion of the Federal STEM Education Strategic Plan.* www.white house.gov/wp-content/uploads/2022/01/2021-CoSTEM-Progress-Report-OSTP.pdf.

Okrent, Abigail and Amy Burke. 2021. "The STEM Labor Force of Today: Scientists, Engineers, and Skilled Technical Workers." National Science Board Science and Engineering Indicators. https://ncses.nsf.gov/pubs/nsb20212.

Oreskes, Naomi. 2019. *Why Trust Science?* Princeton University Press.

Oreskes, Naomi and Eric M. Conway. 2011. *Merchants of Doubt: How a Handful of Scientists Obscured the Truth on Issues from Tobacco Smoke to Global Warming. Bloomsbury Publishing USA.*

Ottinger, Gwen. 2017. "Reconstructing or Reproducing? Scientific Authority and Models of Change in Two Traditions of Citizen Science." In David Tyfield, Rebecca Lave, Samuel Randalls, and Charles Thorpe (eds.), *The Routledge Handbook of the Political Economy of Science.* Routledge, 351–364.

Pardo, Rafael and Félix Calvo. 2004. "The Cognitive Dimension of Public Perceptions of Science: Methodological Issues." *Public Understanding of Science* 13(3): 203–227.

Plaisance, Kathryn S. and Kevin C. Elliott. 2022. "A Framework for Analyzing Broadly Engaged Philosophy of Science." *Philosophy of Science* 88: 594–615. https://doi.org/10.1086/713891.

Potochnik, Angela. 2013. "Defusing Ideological Defenses in Biology." *Bioscience* 63(2): 118–123.

Potochnik, Angela. 2015. "The Diverse Aims of Science." *Studies in History and Philosophy of Science Part A* 53: 71–80.

Potochnik, Angela. 2017. *Idealization and the Aims of Science.* University of Chicago Press.

Potochnik, Angela and Melissa Jacquart. Forthcoming. *Public Engagement with Science: Defining the Project.* Elements in Public Engagement with Science. Cambridge University Press.

Potochnik, Angela, Matteo Colombo, and Cory Wright. 2018. *Recipes for Science: An Introduction to Scientific Methods and Reasoning.* Routledge.

Reichenbach, Hans. 1930. "Kausalität Und Wahrscheinlichkeit." *Erkenntnis* 1: 158–188.

Reisch, George A. 2005. *How the Cold War Transformed the Philosophy of Science: To the Icy Slopes of Logic*. Cambridge University Press.

"Revised Constitution of the Philosophy of Science Association – 1958." 1959. *Philosophy of Science* 26: 63–66.

Romizi, Donata. 2012. "The Vienna Circle's 'Scientific World-Conception': Philosophy of Science in the Political Arena." *Hopos: The Journal of the International Society for the History of Philosophy of Science* 2(2): 205–242.

Sanches de Oliveira, Guilherme and Baggs, Edward. 2023. *Psychologys's WEIRD Problems*. Elements in Psychology and Culture. Cambridge University Press.

Schroeder, Andrew. 2022. "Diversifying Science: Comparing the Benefits of Citizen Science with the Benefits of Bringing More Women into Science." *Synthese* 200: 306. https://doi.org/10.1007/s11229-022-03774-z.

Shirk, Jennifer L., Heidi L. Ballard, Candie C. Wilderman, et al. 2012. "Public Participation in Scientific Research: A Framework for Deliberate Design." *Ecology and Society* 17(2). www.jstor.org/stable/26269051.

Shrader-Frechette, Kristen Sharon. 1994. *Ethics of Scientific Research*. Roman & Littlefield.

Stadler, Friedrich. 2007. "The Vienna Circle: Context, Profile, and Development." In Thomas E. Uebel and Alan W. Richardson (eds.), *The Cambridge Companion to Logical Empiricism*, 13–40. Cambridge University Press.

Stocklmayer, Susan M. and Chris Bryant. 2012. "Science and the Public – What Should People Know?" *International Journal of Science Education, Part B: Communication and Public Engagement* 2(1): 81–101.

Strevens, Michael. 2020. *The Knowledge Machine: How Irrationality Created Modern Science*. 1st ed. Liveright Publishing Corporation.

Swartz, Talia H., Ann-Gel S. Palermo, Sandra K. Masur, and Judith A. Aberg. "The Science and Value of Diversity: Closing the Gaps in Our Understanding of Inclusion and Diversity." *Journal of Infectious Diseases* 220 (Supplement_2): S33–S41.

Uebel, Thomas. 2007. "Philosophy of Social Science in Early Logical Empiricism: The Case of Radical Physicalism." In Thomas E. Uebel and Alan W. Richardson (eds.), *The Cambridge Companion to Logical Empiricism*. Cambridge University Press, 250–277.

Uebel, Thomas E. and Alan W. Richardson (eds.). 2007. *The Cambridge Companion to Logical Empiricism*. Cambridge University Press.

US Senate Committee on Commerce, Science, and Transportation. 2022. "Wicker Praises Research, STEM Education Provisions in New CHIPS

Act," July 22 [press release]. www.commerce.senate.gov/2022/7/wicker-praises-research-stem-education-provisions-in-new-chips-act.

van der Linden, Sander, Anthony Leiserowitz, Seth Rosenthal, and Edward Maibach. 2017. "Inoculating the Public against Misinformation about Climate Change." *Global challenges* 1(2): 1600008. https://doi.org/10.1002/gch2.201600008.

Vaughn, Lisa M. and Farrah Jacquez. 2020. "Participatory Research Methods – Choice Points in the Research Process. *Journal of Participatory Research Methods* 1(1). https://doi.org/10.35844/001c.13244.

Werkmeister, William H. 1936. "The Second International Congress for the Unity of Science." *Philosophical Review* 45(6): 593–600.

Acknowledgments

I owe my deepest thanks for this project to the many people who have helped to develop the Center for Public Engagement in Science (PEWS) at the University of Cincinnati. I have learned so much from their research and insights, and many of my ideas are indelibly shaped by our conversations. This group includes, among others, Ramy Amin, Andrew Bernier, Zvi Biener, Max Cormendy, Amanda Corris, Brooke Crowley, Lucas Dunlap, Andrew Evans, Tim Elmo Feiten, Abel Gustafson, Collin Lucken, Eduardo Martinez, Arnie Miller, Nate Morehouse, Zach Srivastava, Carlie Trott, Taraneh Wilkinson – and most of all, Melissa Jacquart, who is the ideal collaborator in theorizing, teaching, and practicing public engagement with science. Collin Lucken also provided helpful research assistance for this Element.

I'm also grateful for very helpful feedback on the ideas in this work from Kevin Elliott, an anonymous reviewer for Cambridge University Press, and from audiences at presentations at University of Washington, University of California–Irvine, and Science on Tap at Urban Artifact in Cincinnati.

Thanks also to the Taft Research Center at the University of Cincinnati for providing a research fellowship during which I completed this project. Finally, thank you to Jacob Stegenga and Cambridge University Press for this series and for valuable guidance on this project.

Cambridge Elements ≡

Philosophy of Science

Jacob Stegenga
University of Cambridge
Jacob Stegenga is a Reader in the Department of History and Philosophy of Science
at the University of Cambridge. He has published widely on fundamental topics in reason-
ing and rationality and philosophical problems in medicine and biology. Prior to joining
Cambridge he taught in the United States and Canada, and he received his PhD from the
University of California–San Diego.

About the Series

This series of Elements in Philosophy of Science provides an extensive overview of the
themes, topics and debates which constitute the philosophy of science. Distinguished
specialists provide an up-to-date summary of the results of current research on their
topics, as well as offering their own take on those topics and drawing original
conclusions.

Cambridge Elements $\equiv$

Philosophy of Science

Printed in the USA
CPSIA information can be obtained
at www.ICGtesting.com
LVHW011118310724
786976LV00004B/419

9 781009 048828